MINDBENDERS
AND
BRAINTEASERS

MINDBENDERS AND BRAINTEASERS

GYLES BRANDRETH
&
TREVOR TRURAN

CHANCELLOR
PRESS

First published in Great Britain by Octopus Books Ltd
in two separate volumes entitled
Masterful Mindbenders and *Puzzles and Brainteasers*.

This one-volume collection first published in 1987 by
Treasure Press an imprint of Reed Consumer Books Limited
Michelin House
81 Fulham Road
London SW3 6RB
and Auckland, Melbourne, Singapore and Toronto

© 1984 and 1982 Hennerwood Productions

ISBN 1 85152 522 X

A CIP catalogue record for this book is available at the
British Library

Printed & bound in Great Britain
by HarperCollins, Glasgow

TREVOR TRURAN'S
MASTERFUL MINDBENDERS

INTRODUCTION

The aim in offering these puzzles is to amuse and entertain and not to baffle with specialist knowledge, complex chains of thought or devious tricks. There are ten chapters which will keep you happily occupied in various ways without, it is hoped, too much mental strain. The puzzles are graded ? to ??? to give you a rough idea of the level of difficulty (? being the easiest and ??? the toughest) so that you can make a selection according to age or inclination.

Now, off you go and enjoy a mind-bending experience!

ODD MAN OUT

Can you spot the one black sheep in each family? In most cases, the trick is to work out what joins the rest together. Only simple general knowledge and powers of observation are required here.

In any group there is always one 'odd man out' — at parties it is usually me. Who else can enter a roomful of evening dress and glittering jewellery without taking his bicycle clips off; kiss the back of his hostess's hand — the one holding the glass of champagne — and tell the vicar that if he'd known it was fancy dress he would have turned up as Henry VIII?

The trouble with any gathering is that it is always possible, in a negative way, to make any one member the odd one out. A quick flash of the optics over

HAT COAT GLOVE SHOE UMBRELLA SCARF

and you could say that SHOE is the odd one out as none of the others are, usually, worn on the feet. Ditto any of the others for a variety of reasons.

What is missing here is, if SHOE does not belong, what *positive* link is there which connects all the others but which still excludes SHOE?

In looking at the list it is better, perhaps, to look for the link which joins all but one of the members together — in this case HAT, GLOVE, COAT, SHOE, SCARF are all *worn* — an UMBRELLA isn't.

In the puzzles which follow, award yourself 3 points for every answer you give which agrees with our solution and, as a special sale offer, 1 point for any other answer you come up with, which you can convince a *sensible* friend is correct!

1(?)

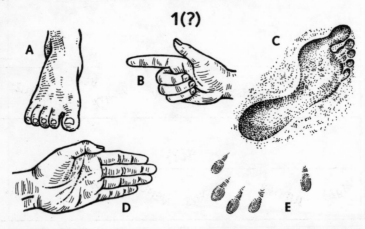

2(?)

THIRTYSIX   NINE   EIGHTYONE   FIFTYFOUR   ONE   TWENTYFIVE
FOUR

3(?)

4(?)

BROWN   PINK   RED   YELLOW   GREEN   BLACK   WHITE   BLUE   ORANGE

5(?)

MARS   JUPITER   URANUS   VENUS   SATURN   NEPTUNE

SOLUTIONS ON PAGES 169 AND 170.

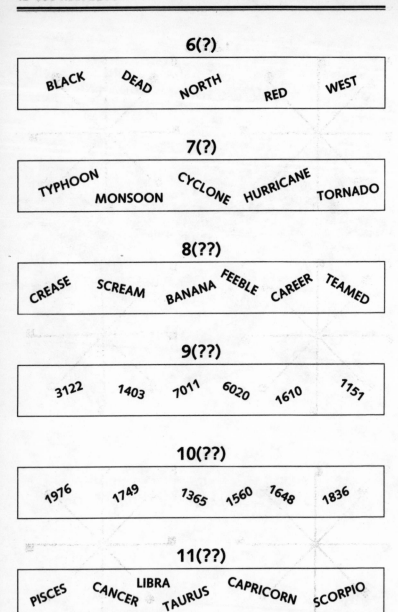

6(?)

BLACK   DEAD   NORTH   RED   WEST

7(?)

TYPHOON   MONSOON   CYCLONE   HURRICANE   TORNADO

8(??)

CREASE   SCREAM   BANANA   FEEBLE   CAREER   TEAMED

9(??)

3122   1403   7011   6020   1610   1151

10(??)

1976   1749   1365   1560   1648   1836

11(??)

PISCES   CANCER   LIBRA   TAURUS   CAPRICORN   SCORPIO

SOLUTIONS ON PAGES 169 AND 170.

12(??)

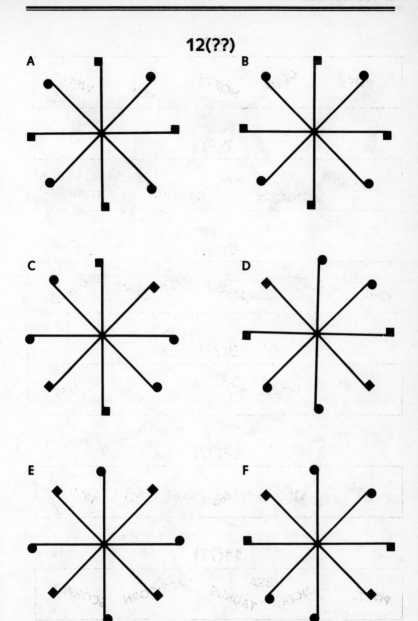

SOLUTION ON PAGE 170.

13(??)

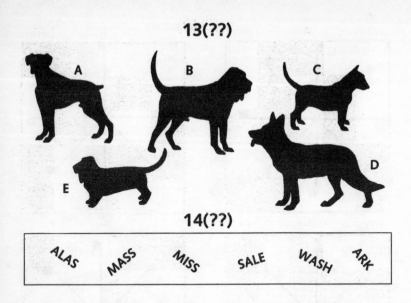

14(??)

| ALAS | MASS | MISS | SALE | WASH | ARK |

15(???)

JAMES   MICHAEL   EDWARD   HAROLD   ALEC   ANTHONY

16(???)

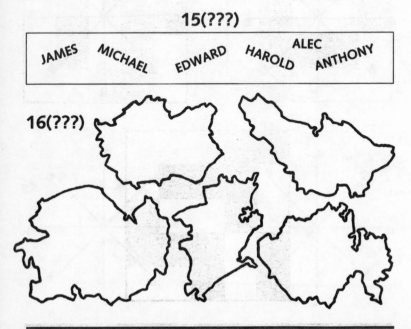

17(???)

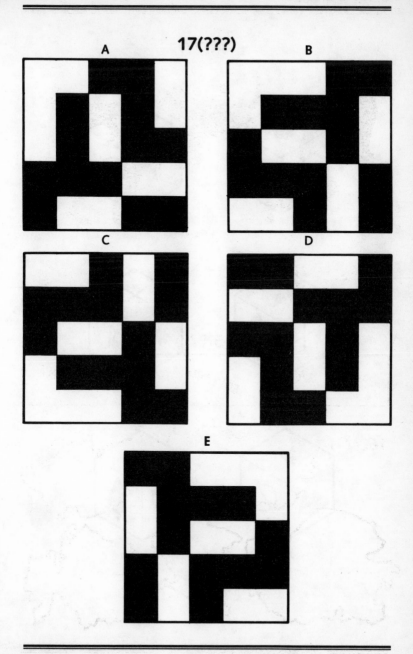

A

B

C

D

E

SOLUTION ON PAGE 170.

18(???)

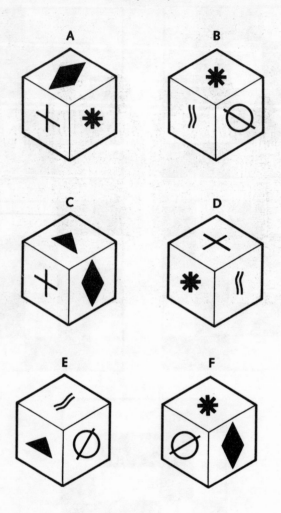

19(???)

20(???)

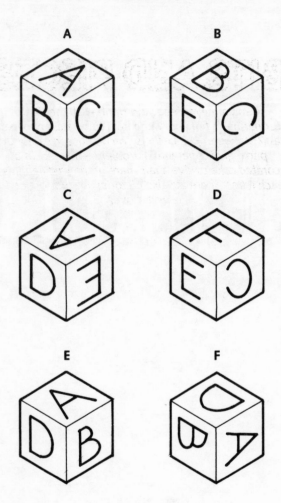

SOLUTION ON PAGE 169.

BITS AND PIECES

Can your eyes feed your brain with the right information to tell your hand how to be a cut above the rest? Strawberry Shares lets you practise in safety the party-giver's perennial problem – how to cut a decorated cake to give a fair share of the iced delights to each eater. There are also pictorial puzzles for you to ponder over.

Half-Caked Idea (?)

Mrs Little had a problem. Whenever she had a cake to share between her two children, the arguments as to who should have which piece made the neighbours think World War Three had started early.

However carefully she made the cut, when she served up the pieces both children would protest that their 'half' was smaller.

One day she had an idea. She called the children into the kitchen, stood them beside the table where the cake and the cake knife lay and said something which at once put an end to all argument.
What did she tell the children to do, so that neither could complain about the share of cake each received?

Strawberry Shares (? & ??)

The neat solution to the last puzzle becomes impossible when the cake has to be cut into several pieces and the cake has been brightly decorated. Everybody has to have an equal share of the cake and many a gimlet eye will be fixed on the server to make sure they do not miss out on a star, a strawberry or a blob of cream.

To increase your skill in this difficult art we have asked a master chef to prepare a dozen decorated delights, enough for a jubilee street party.

He has carefully added lines made from hundreds and thousands along which the cake can be cut.

In each case, every person must have an equal sized share — though they do not have to have the same shape as each other. And each must have the same number of each decoration as everybody else.
Can you draw in the lines to show how the cake should be divided up?
(Hint — if each person has, say, just one star then where two stars are next to each other there must be a cut along the line between them — fill these lines in first and the rest will be, dare we say it, a piece of cake!)

SOLUTION ON PAGE 169.

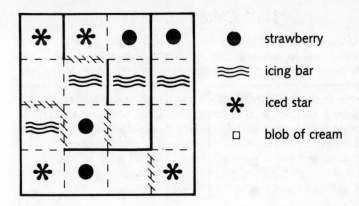

●	strawberry
≋	icing bar
✳	iced star
□	blob of cream

4 pieces 1 iced star, 1 icing bar, 1 strawberry in each piece. There must be a cut wherever the same symbols are in adjacent squares. There can only be one empty square in each piece as well so there must be a cut where empty squares are next door. The hatch line shows how the cutting must be completed.

ONE

6 pieces 1 iced star, 1 icing bar, 1 strawberry in each.

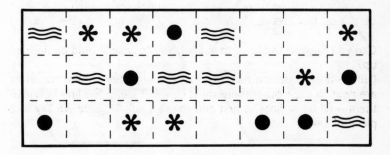

SOLUTION ON PAGE 171.

TWO

6 pieces 1 star, 1 bar,
1 strawberry in each.

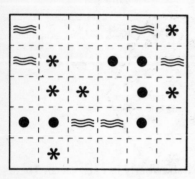

THREE

6 pieces 2 stars, 1 bar,
1 strawberry in each.

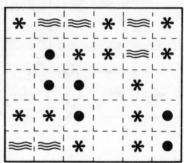

FOUR

6 pieces 1 star, 1 bar in each.

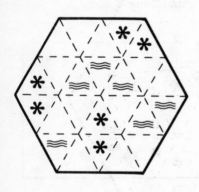

FIVE

6 pieces 1 star, 1 bar,
1 strawberry in each.

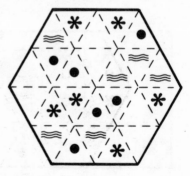

SOLUTIONS ON PAGES 171, 172 and 173.

SIX

3 pieces 3 stars, 1 bar, 3 strawberries in each.

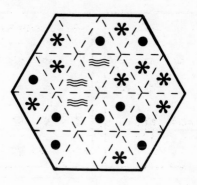

SEVEN

9 pieces 1 star, 1 bar, 1 strawberry, 2 blobs of cream in each.

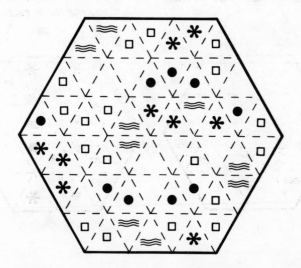

EIGHT

12 pieces 1 star, 1 bar, 1 strawberry in each.

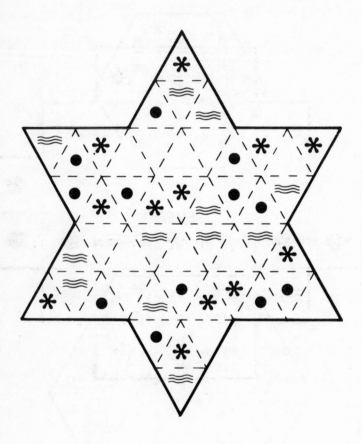

SOLUTION ON PAGE 173.

NINE

5 pieces 1 star, 1 bar, 2 strawberries, 1 blob of cream in each.

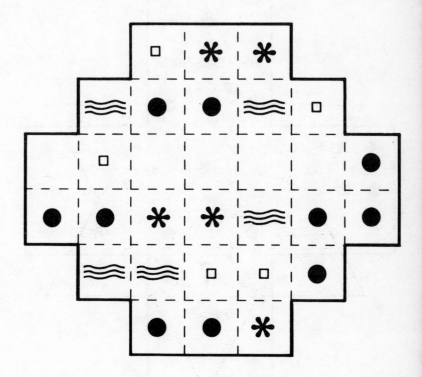

TEN

9 pieces 1 star, 1 bar, 1 strawberry, 1 blob of cream in each.

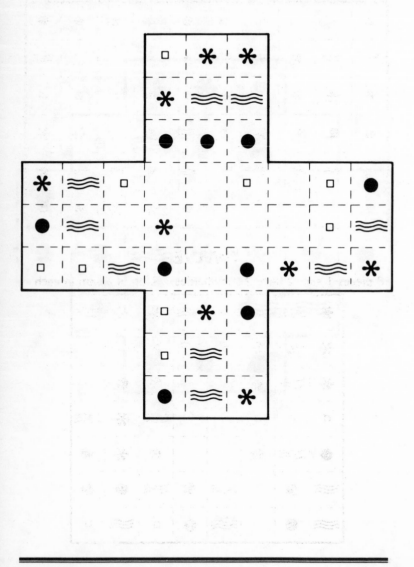

SOLUTION ON PAGE 171.

ELEVEN

12 pieces 1 star, 1 bar, 2 strawberries in each.

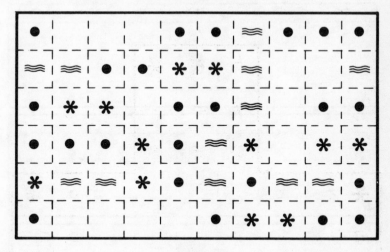

TWELVE

8 pieces 1 star, 2 bars, 2 strawberries, 1 blob of cream in each.

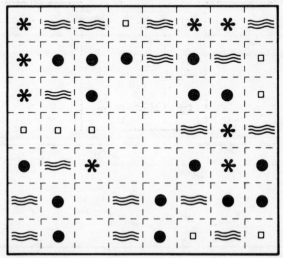

In Sequence (?)

Can you put these five pictures into the correct order?

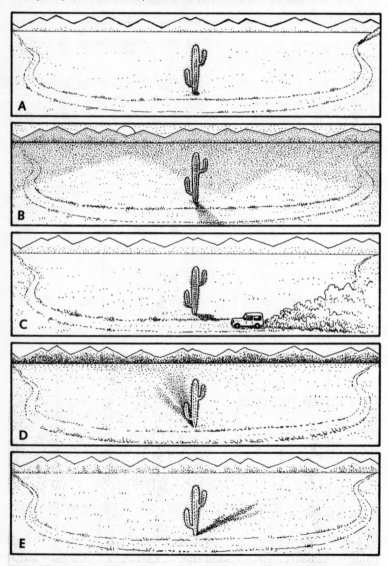

SOLUTION ON PAGE 174.

Party Pieces (?)

These five snaps of Lady Amelia's garden party last summer have been muddled up. Can you work out the order in which they were taken?

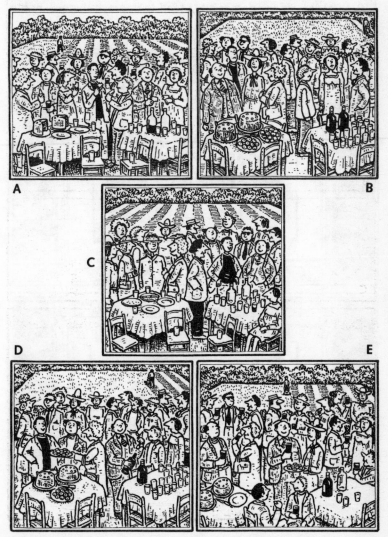

A

B

C

D

E

SOLUTION ON PAGE 174.

Spot The Difference (?)

When young Justus Thumb tried to break the local arcade's Space Invaders machine record the local press photographer took a picture.

Back at the office another artist tried to improve the quality but made 20 mistakes.

How many of them can you spot?

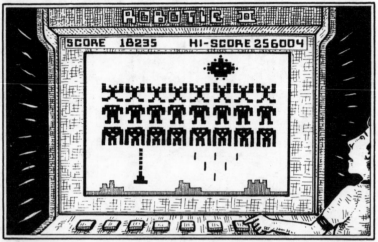

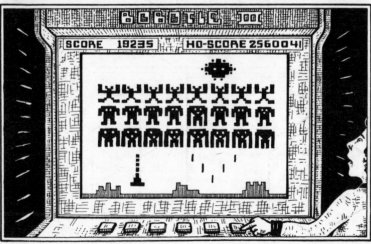

SOLUTION ON PAGE 173.

Cube Bits (??)

A $2 \times 2 \times 2$ cube is to be made from eight unit cubes. Each face of the big cube will be entirely in one of the six colours. The faces of the unit cubes which touch inside the big cube will be black.
Can the big cube be made with these eight small cubes?

Any face on a small cube which you cannot see is black.

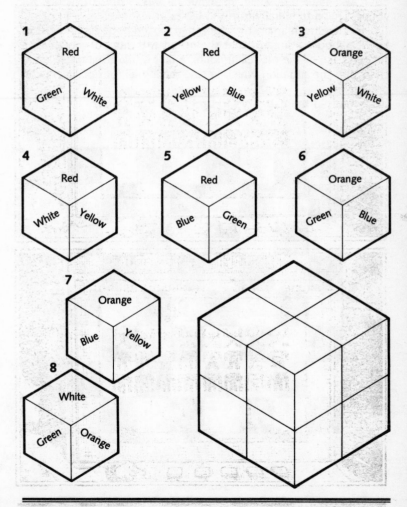

1 Red / Green / White

2 Red / Yellow / Blue

3 Orange / Yellow / White

4 Red / White / Yellow

5 Red / Blue / Green

6 Orange / Green / Blue

7 Orange / Blue / Yellow

8 White / Green / Orange

SOLUTION ON PAGE 174.

The Winning Cut (??)

While Mrs Little is busy making more cakes, Mr Little is learning a bitter lesson — that children play to their own rules and that buying cheap can be a mistake.

Like the draughts board and pieces made from felt and cut from the packet with a modelling knife.

It was cheap, quick and easy — just as the advert had promised. But it also made it possible, just when he was assured of victory, for young Cheryl to literally turn the tables at a stroke.

Her one Queen against his four men looked hopeless and just as he was about to suggest that she resign with honour there was a sudden flash of the modelling knife, a blur of hands and felt and a change in the situation which left her taking all four of his men in one move!

Just what did the naughty girl do to win that game?

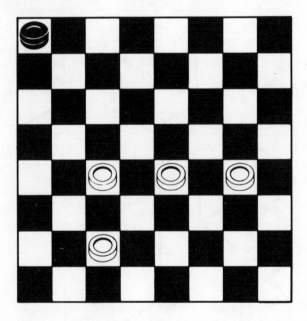

BLACK: Cheryl   **WHITE: Dad**

SOLUTION ON PAGE 174.

RIDDLES

Strike up the band, lift the curtain, sit back and indulge in a host of entertaining jokes, stories, verses and strange situations. You are also invited to take part in the famous head-to-head confrontation, What's My Blank?

What's My Blank (? & ??)

In this little word puzzle, derived from a certain TV programme which you may have seen, you will be given a series of clues, like blank something or something blank. You are then invited to make your choice of one of the several possibilities which may occur to you.

If you make the right choice of answers, then the initial letters will spell out yet another word — and that is the solution you are seeking.

To make the thing a bit easier you have a couple of clues:

1 The length of the missing word is given or here and there the middle letters may already be in place.
2 A cryptic clue is offered to the solution word.

In case you are still feeling a bit blank yourself, cast a spare eye or two over this example.

Note: the number of blanks in this type of puzzle equals the number of letters.

----- bank	B	lood
----- ---- cabin	U	ncle Tom's
----- rose	T	udor
--- leaf	T	ea
---- due	O	ver
Bird's ----	N	est

Clue: Connected with clothing.
So the answer is button.

Sometimes the answer will be not one but two words, one given by the initial letters and the other by the last letters of the answers. These two words will always have a strong association, as do CAT NAP, the solution to the example at the top of the next page.

Note: the number of blanks in this type of puzzle does not equal the number of letters.

Tin -----	C	a	N
----- bet!	A	lph	A
----- door	T	ra	P

Clue: What a domestic pet may have.

ONE (?)

---- handed	
Treasure ------	
Special -----	
Royal ----	

Clue: An animal.

TWO (?)

Solar -----	
Soft ------	
------ apple	
Marble ----	
--- nail	
Blood ------	

Clue: A vegetable.

SOLUTIONS ON PAGE 174.

THREE (?)

------ ticket	
---- duckling	
--- meter	
----- sauce	
--- doll	

Clue: Bought at the grocer's.

FOUR (?)

----- top		LIF
----- shower		PRI
Dr -----		
Evening -----		RES
Light -----		EAR

Clue: Part of the fun of the fair.

FIVE (?)

First -----		LAS
----- street		IG
Look -----		NT
Bicycle -----		UM

Clue: Where you find newspapers and grease.

SOLUTIONS ON PAGE 174.

SIX (?)

Sweet -----		
Hammer and -----		
Arabian ------		
---- washer		
------ whale		
----- time		
---- up		
----- line		
Water ----		
---- worm		
------ parade		
Green -------		

Clue: You carry it around in your pocket.

SEVEN (?)

----- glass	IN	
----- tube	NNE	
----- rash	ETTL	
----- piece	Y	

Clue: Grows in the countryside.

EIGHT (??)

New ---- □
Jet ------ □
Wedding ---- □
Space -------- □
---- book □
---- post □
Down ----- □
--- ache □

Clue: Something sweet to eat.

A Fir Question (?)

Which film hero wrote this in his newspaper?

> My start rhymes with blue,
> My middle with fir.
> My end rhymes with can
> A clue? – south coast county.
> Tell me, who must I be?

Gardeners' Question Time (?)

My one, two, three takes you far and wide.
My two, three, four, say, in short, you've arrived.
My four, five, six means to decompose
My whole is a food the gardener grows.

What am I?

SOLUTIONS ON PAGES 174 AND 175.

One, Two, Three ... (?)

My one is in ONE but not in TWO.
My two is in TWO but not in THREE.
My three is in THREE but not in FOUR.
My whole can be seen on hill and moor.

What am I?

Calling All Puzzlers (?)

Some of the letters in each line of our coded message, taken in the order they appear, spell a word whose length is given by the number in brackets at the end. Thus AX<u>T</u>GY<u>E</u>S<u>M</u><u>T</u> (4) would give the word TEST.

If you can find the word in each line a phrase useful to all readers of this book will appear.

KALDEFT (3)   ETAJSSKFNE (4)
YMOPNGURT (4)   PLQMOZTLXHKE (3)
VAPBORZTAINFZ (5)   SMPEEFGTROOAOTINLLY (5)

Crashword (?)

The clues are entered one letter to each square but, as you can see from the letters, they overlap a bit – rather like a line of cars which didn't stop as quickly as the first one. The result is a household object – can you find out what it is?

(**a**) Is in the past.   (**d**) Short raincoat.
(**b**) Below the knee.   (**e**) Facial feature.
(**c**) Letter of force.   (**f**) Isle Of Wight feature.

Jungle Jester (?)

My first is in March but not in hare.
My second in lion but not in lair.
My third in money can be found.
My fourth in sky-high but not in sound.
My fifth and sixth in every and year.
My whole fills the jungle with noise and cheer.

What am I?

Headless Rhyme (?)

here as a oung an rom ee
ho ent or a wim n he ea.
A hark aw is lippers
nd aid 'hoopee ippers!'
hen te he oung an or is ea.

This should have been, Jones the Word thought, a winner at the Sillybillyogogogog Eisteddfod. If only Dai the Print hadn't missed off the first letter of every word which had 2 or more letters in it.

It hadn't been much of a help, though a kind thought, when Dai printed all the missing letters at the bottom of the page; the judges were too far gone to sort it out.

Can you put the letters where they belong and make sense of Jones' masterpiece?

A, A, D, F, F, F, F, H, H, I, K, M, M, S, S, S, S, S, T, T, T, T, T, W, W, W, W, Y, Y.

The Story So Far... (?)

The school magazine was not coming along too well. It had seemed a good idea to form 3K to start one, especially the idea of writing adventure stories in which they were the main characters.

The problem was in the production side; it is difficult for the typesetter to get the text right when the features editor uses the rubber printing outfit as ammunition against the sports editor.

SOLUTIONS ON PAGE 176.

Quite near to tears, the editor stared at the mangled text:

> T . . . . y S . . . t and her fri . . . ., Chris . . . her and S . . . ra
>
> Ed . . . ds, ... fully t . . . ed the key to the w . . . house
>
> door. S . . . ly it began to open, g . . . . ing and g . . . ling
>
> like a bear d . . tur . . d dur . . g it w . . ter s . . . p.
>
>   Inside the d . . . ness c . . . ded around our s . . . ed
>
> heroes; s . . . . ering noises . . . their teeth c . . . . . . ing in
>
> f . . . . . . So . . where in this v . . t buil . . . g the c . . . . s had
>
> st . . . ed the g . . . bul . . . . .
>
> As they g . . . . d t . . ir way along a m . . ty, s . . lly w . . ., a
>
> s . . . ch c . . . . ed on and a br . . . iant sh . . . of light p . . . ed
>
> on them.
>
>   They were t . . . ped!

With a long sigh the editor, true to her noble calling, crawled around the classroom floor until she had picked up all the missing pieces. She arranged them neatly on her table and began to wonder where each fitted.

> aft all and are ark as ash be camp car care cot din ends
> hatter he ill in in is lay lee lick lion low me me old race rap
> right roan rook rope row row set top urn us war wit

Can you lend a hand and put the short words back where they belong and save the magazine from disaster?

SOLUTION ON PAGE 176.

Film Fun (?)

Very often it is the catchy title of a film which makes it a box office sensation. There are many films which might have been famous except for a flaw in the title.

Can you name them from these brief outlines of their plots?

The final test match at Lords. A batsman has survived several calls for leg before wicket and is playing very slowly and boring everybody.

He eventually hits the ball hard and straight. No fielder touches the ball but suddenly it flies back and hits the batsman on the nose.

After years and years standing in salt water the piles of Bournemouth Pier have become soft and supple.

One night the pier becomes alive, tries its legs and walks out to sea!

After many adventures under the oceans of the world it comes back home again.

It is St David's Day, 1942. A convoy of 10 ships, each carrying 2,000 Welshmen returning to the land of their fathers after years in America, is ploughing across the ocean.

It is attacked by a German submarine and all the ships are sunk, with the loss of all the men.

At the children's birthday party all is laughter and fun — especially when a rather severe-looking nanny produces a hatpin and bursts all the balloons.

The Film of the Film!
A British spy escapes from the Kremlin with a handy object which is urgently needed at Shepperton Studios where the making of another Bond film is held up due to Arctic conditions.

(As well as the film title from this story, what film was being made at Shepperton?)

SOLUTION ON PAGE 175.

What Is It? (?)

There are those who think that it is flat
Though most think it is round.
To be closer still, it's tangerine-shaped
And on it you can be drowned!

What's Yours? (?)

Some keep theirs in the garden.
Some have theirs indoors.
Some are found under water.
Tell me – have you made yours?

The Place To Be (?)

My first is in fat but not in thin.
My next in wide but not in trim.
My third in old but not in young.
My fourth and fifth in large not small.
My sixth (and seventh!) in noise and sound.
My whole the place where you may be found.

A Word From The Bard (?)

First, it runs through field and town,
Never goes up, always goes down.
Then lifts and falls for many a day
'Til it climbs to the sky up, up and away.
It floats on high and puts on weight
Then falls once more at quite a rate.
When hot it's thin; when cold its hard.
So what is the subject of this bard?

Spot This One (?)

What has 21 spots but isn't ill?

Get This (?)

What's full of holes and gets hit with clubs?

SOLUTIONS ON PAGE 175.

Bleep, Bleep (?)

What's empty and tears round and round going 'bleep, bleep, fire! Bleep, bleep, fire!'?

Across The Great Divide (??)

Spare, if you will, a thought for Edwina Proud
Who now strums a harp on a heavenly cloud.
She died, at peace, on a recent Monday
But was laid in her grave on the PREVIOUS Sunday!

No crime or error attended this act.
So can you explain the incredible fact
That the lady died at half past four
And then was buried the day before?!

Codesquare (??)

The letters of the alphabet have been scattered about and cast forth upon the numbers 1 to 9. Thus the number 1 in the picture on the right can be either N, D or I. In the square, the same number always stands for the same letter so, like the ancient mariner who picketh one in three, can you find out which number stands for which letter and complete the word square with five words reading the same across and down?

1 D I N		**2** E C Q
3 T V P		**4** W U S
5 M G B		**6** A Y F
7 K L J		**8** Z R H
9 X O		

4	3	6	8	3
3	2	1	9	8
6	1	5	7	2
8	9	7	2	4
3	8	2	4	4

Codeword (???)

It may not look much like it but the picture overleaf really is a crossword grid. There are words going across and down and blank squares scattered here, there and probably somewhere else as well. All we have done is to replace the letters by a number and you can see that each number is shared by 2 letters. So the number 1 may be a or it may be b (try saying that ten times quickly!).

The blank has been coded by one of the numbers as well – and every blank does at least have the same number.

In case this looks harder than it really is, don't forget that after every word which does not end at the edge of the grid is a blank square. There must also be a blank square before each word which does not start at an edge.

SOLUTION ON PAGE 176.

Given all that help, can you now put each of the following words into its one correct position?

ABBA ACE ADDED AGE AHEAD BAD BADGE BEACH BEECH CADGE CHAFE CHEF DACE DEAF DECIDE DEFACE DI EACH EGG EH FACE FED FEE FIG HA HAD HEED HI IBID IDE IE IF JABBED JADE

2	3	3	1	2	3	4	4	5	1	5	2
3	4	3	4	1	4	3	1	2	4	4	4
1	2	2	3	2	4	4	1	3	1	2	4
3	4	4	1	4	3	4	1	4	4	4	1
4	3	1	2	3	4	5	1	1	1	3	2
4	5	4	4	4	4	1	4	3	4	3	4
3	4	4	4	1	1	2	4	3	4	4	3
3	4	4	2	1	2	3	4	2	4	5	3
2	3	2	5	2	3	4	2	4	1	3	3

$$\begin{aligned}
\mathbf{1} &= \text{A or B} & \mathbf{2} &= \text{C or D} \\
\mathbf{3} &= \text{E or F} & \mathbf{4} &= \text{G or H} \\
\mathbf{5} &= \text{I or J}
\end{aligned}$$

SOLUTION ON PAGE 175.

WHO DID WHAT?

Can you put the separate statements together and make the right deduction? For example . . . Henry drove the red car. The yellow van went over the cliff . . . So Henry, whatever fate befell him, did not make that long fall into the sea. Once you have found who didn't do what, you will discover who did. If using the grids is new to you, the chapter opens with a sample which is worked through completely to help you follow the method.

Stand in a load of stolen cement.

Have you done a Who Did What-type puzzle before? If so, turn to page 53. If not, read on. Here is the problem:

Five youngsters each played a different game on five different arcade machines. They scored five different totals as well but all we can recall is that

1. Teresa played Crunch and scored more than 5,000 but did not get the top score.
2. A boy played on the Marvel and a girl scored 6,000 playing Splat on the Quasar.
3. Thud was played on the Pinball.
4. Peter did not score as high as 10,000 which was made on the Wizard.
5. Phillip played Zap and he did not score less than 6,000.
6. Pow was not played by Steven and did not produce the lowest score.
7. The highest score was made on the Freakout.

The puzzle is to work out who played which game on which machine for how many points.

You could put all the facts together in your brain and let it churn around until, hopefully, it coughs up the answer like a Try Your Weight machine at the seaside. If all it does is make your head ache, then our grid may prove helpful.

It shows all the possible combinations which the puzzle throws up and can be filled in by putting a tick where a pair is proved to go together and a cross when the pairing is not possible.

As the grid is filled in, other facts will emerge like the cork out of a bottle of shaken champagne.

	Zap	Pow	Thud	Crunch	Splat	Quasar	Wizard	Pinball	Freakout	Marvel	3000	5000	6000	10 000	12 000
Alison				X₁											
Peter				X₁											
Teresa	X₁	X₁	X₁	✓₁	X₁						X₁	X₁			X₁
Phillip				X₁											
Steven				X₁											
Quasar															
Wizard															
Pinball															
Freakout															
Marvel															
3000				X₁											
5000				X₁											
6000															
10 000															
12 000				X₁											

Clue 1: Put a tick for Teresa playing Crunch and a cross for all the others not playing that game. Teresa/Crunch has a score greater than 5,000 but not the top score, so put a cross for that score and less and a cross against 12,000, the top score.

	Zap	Pow	Thud	Crunch	Splat	Quasar	Wizard	Pinball	Freakout	Marvel	3000	5000	6000	10 000	12 000
Alison	X₂	X₂	X₂	X	✓₂	✓₂	X₂	X₂	X₂	X₂	X₂	X₂	✓₂	X₂	X₂
Peter				X	X₂	X₂							X₂	X₂	
Teresa	X	X	X	✓	X	X₂				X₂	X	X	X₂	✓₂	X
Phillip				X	X₂	X₂							X₂	X₂	
Steven				X	X₂	X₂							X₂	X₂	
Quasar	X₂	X₂	X₂	X₂	✓₂										
Wizard					X₂										
Pinball					X₂										
Freakout					X₂										
Marvel				X₂	X₂										
3000				X	X₂										
5000				X	X₂										
6000	X₂	X₂	X₂	X₂	✓₂										
10 000	X₂	X₂	X₂	✓₂	X₂										
12 000				X	X₂										

Clue 2: A boy played on the Marvel so put a cross against each girl and the Marvel. From clue 1 we know a girl played Crunch so put a cross against Crunch/Marvel. A girl played Splat giving a cross against each boy and that game. This only leaves Alison, so she played Splat – a tick for that. It was played on the Quasar, so tick (and consequent crosses) record that fact. From this Teresa is only left with one possible score, 10,000, so tick that.

	Zap	Pow	Thud	Crunch	Splat	Quasar	Wizard	Pinball	Freakout	Marvel	3000	5000	6000	10 000	12 000
Alison	X	X	X	X	✓	✓	X	X	X	X	X	X	✓	X	X
Peter				X	X	✓	X₄						X	X	X₄
Teresa	X	X	X	✓	X	X	✓₄	X₃	X₄	X	X	X	X	✓	X
Phillip				X	X	✓	X₄						X	X	
Steven				X	X	✓	X₄						X	X	
Quasar	X	X	X	X	✓										
Wizard	X₄	X₄	X₃	✓₄	X										
Pinball	X₃	X₃	✓₃	X₃	X										
Freakout			X₃	X₄	X										
Marvel			X₃	X	X										
3000				X	X										
5000				X	X										
6000	X	X	X	X	✓										
10 000	X	X	X	✓	X										
12 000				X	X										

Clue 3: Tick Thud/Pinball and cross the impossibles. Teresa did not play Thud, so put a cross against Teresa/Pinball.

Clue 4: Cross out Peter/12,000. Teresa is known already to have scored 10,000, so she played on the Wizard.

	Zap	Pow	Thud	Crunch	Splat	Quasar	Wizard	Pinball	Freakout	Marvel	3000	5000	6000	10 000	12 000
Alison	X	X	X	X	✓	✓	X	X	X	X	X	X	✓	X	X
Peter	X₅	✓₆	X₆	X	X	X	X	X₆	X₇	✓₇	X₆	✓₆	X	X	X
Teresa	X	X	X	✓	X	X	X	X	X	X	X	X	X	✓	X
Phillip	✓₅	X₅	X₅	X	X	X	X	X₅	✓₇	X₇	X₅	X₅	X	X	✓₅
Steven	X₅	X₆	✓₆	X	X	X	X	✓₆	X₆	X₆	✓₆	X₆	✓	X	X₅
Quasar	X	X	X	X	✓										
Wizard	X	X	X	✓	X										
Pinball	X	X	✓	X	X										
Freakout			X	X	X										
Marvel			X	X	X										
3000	X₅			X	X										
5000	X₅			X	X										
6000	X	X	X	X	✓										
10 000	X	X	X	✓	X										
12 000	✓₅	X₅	X₅	X	X										

Clue 5: Tick Phillip/Zap. Cross out Phillip scoring less than 6,000. This only leaves him with 12,000, so tick that. Phillip, by clue 3, could not have played on the Pinball, so cross that out.

Clue 6: Pow was not played by Steven, so that is crossed out and this only leaves him with Thud so tick that, and it is already known that that was played on the Pinball – another tick. This leaves Peter Playing Pow. He did not get the lowest score, so he scored 5,000 which leaves only Steven with 3,000.

Clue 7: Phillip was playing on the Freakout as he made the highest score. All of which leaves Peter on the Marvel and the solution is complete.

Alison	Splat	Quasar	6,000
Peter	Pow	Marvel	5,000
Teresa	Crunch	Wizard	10,000
Phillip	Zap	Freakout	12,000
Steven	Thud	Pinball	3,000

OI! WHAT IS THE FAVOURITE DISH AT TARZAN'S JUNGLE CAFE?

A snake and pygmy pie.

The Seaside Saga (?)

So excited were the four children on their way home on the coach that they chattered nonstop about their excursion to Sheermouth.

When the last had been dropped off, tiredly clutching the hand of the grown up who had taken him, the driver parked his coach and went home to tell his wife what a day they had all had.

She, naturally, wanted all the details but, being a good driver, he had concentrated on the road and could only remember a few snatches of conversation.

He knew that each child had had one special treat and had been with only one adult. He also remembered that:

The uncle had paid for the donkey ride.

Brian had eaten the ice cream, which a man had bought for him.

Tim did not go to the funfair and Sarah did not go on the donkey ride or with her aunt.

Mother took her daughter to the funfair while Tim went with his aunt.

The driver's wife tried to work out just which of the children had enjoyed which treat with which adult, but she became muddled and gave up.

Can you sort it out for her using the grid on the next page?

	Donkey Ride	Ice Cream	Funfair	Pier	Mother	Grandad	Uncle	Aunt
Sarah								
Brian								
Tim								
Joan								
Mother					
Grandad					
Uncle					
Aunt					

Name	Treat	Who with
Sarah		
Brian		
Tim		
Joan		

Minor League (?)

For the local correspondent of the *Much Squelching Argus and Ferret Gazette*, reporting the new basketball league which had sprung up in the village hall proved an unrewarding task.

Due more to lack of skill on the part of the exuberant youngsters rather than actual malice, he found himself involved in the game as ball-catcher, usually on the tip of the nose. The excited yelling of four teams of youngsters, whose one ambition in life was to become seven feet tall, was a far cry from the weddings and council meetings which were his usual function.

Late that night, as he nursed two eyes which refused to work as a team, he tried to make some sense of his notes on the season just ended.

Bill's team finished higher in the league than Tony's team and the Allstars.

Leslie's team finished third.

Bluesox finished bottom of the league.

Fred played for the Giants who came second.

Can you give him a mental hand and list the four teams, their star player and where each finished the season?

	Allstars	Giants	Bluesox	Bears	1	2	3	4
Bill								
Fred								
Leslie								
Tony								
1				
2				
3				
4				

Name	Team	Position
Bill		
Fred		
Leslie		
Tony		

SOLUTION ON PAGE 176.

Ring O Rose's (?)

This delightful snap taken at the Happyhour Playgroup just before the ice cream and cakes started flying shows six children standing with their best friend on one side and their sibling on the other. (Sibling is a lovely word which means brother or sister – if you happen to have one under six months old it is your dribbling sibling!)

Now Colin's friend's brother is Edward.

Edward's friend is not Sarah.

Rose's brother's friend is Edward's sister.

Can you work out who is next to whom and so write each toddler's name by their picture?

Girls: Rose, Sarah, Tanya
Boys: Andrew, Colin, Edward

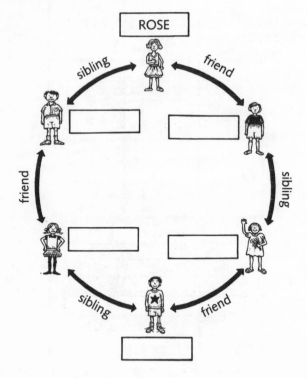

Fruit & Veg. (?)

For young Ted the youth opportunity scheme meant little more than humping great bags of potatoes around and constantly rearranging the display to suit the everchanging demands of his boss, Mr Squashett.

Ted's latest task is to present six fruits and six vegetables in a stand of three rows.

Old Squashie's commands were that fruit and veg. were to alternate across and down so that two fruits or two vegetables were never next to each other.

The oranges were to be directly above the cucumbers which were to be on the left of the grapes.

The sprouts must be above the pears; the plums directly above the cabbage and the apples in between the lettuce and the sprouts.

The cucumbers were to be in the bottom row on the right of the peaches.

The potatoes were to be in the bottom right corner, in the same column as the sprouts.

So just where did Ted put the carrots?

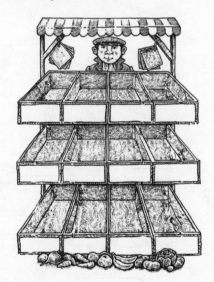

SOLUTION ON PAGE 177.

Road Up (?)

The Merrivale traffic census did a splendid job in proving what is known already, that there are too many cars using too few roads.

What they failed to record was who lived in which road but the record does show that:

The Sangsters went down as many roads as the Hughes' to reach the High Street.

Miss Briscoe used Fuller Vale to reach the High Street but the Dennetts' journey did not take them this way.

Mr Adams went down more roads to reach the High Street than Mrs Ready who went down more roads than Mr & Mrs Thomas, who lived in Fairfield Road.

Miss Briscoe turned right to leave the road she lived in, then right again to reach Mrs Ready's house which is in the next road to the Hughes family.

Can you complete the census form – posterity may need it!

(The number by each house in our helpful map gives the number of roads used to reach the High Street from each house.)

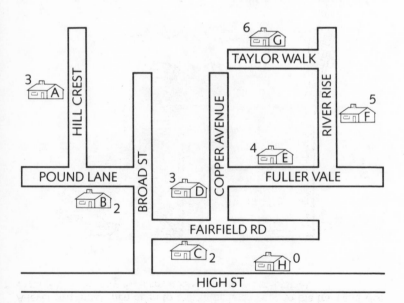

SOLUTION ON PAGE 176.

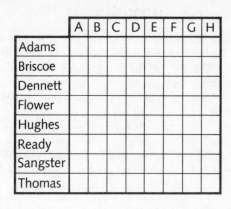

	A	B	C	D	E	F	G	H
Adams								
Briscoe								
Dennett								
Flower								
Hughes								
Ready								
Sangster								
Thomas								

ANSWER ME THIS: WHAT IS OPEN WHEN IT IS SHUT AND SHUT WHEN IT IS OPEN?

A level crossing. When open to the traffic it is closed to the train and vice versa. (Also, country dwellers, a kissing gate is acceptable).

Take It From Here (??)

It was a mistake, the residents of Carrington Crescent later agreed, to let young Tim earn extra pocket money by sending him with a block order for five dinners to the Chinese takeaway in the High Street. Not that he disappeared with the money or dropped the order over the canal bridge on his way back. It was simply that between his forgetfulness and the shop owner's limited command of English, the result was one large and very mixed packet of foodstuffs and an order form sinking for the third time in a sea of sweet and sour sauce. As he dived, unseen, into the garage of Number 3, he had his facts as tangled as a plate of spaghetti.

Dora Innis had ordered number 21 and Mr Goldsmith wanted the special.

Charles, whose surname isn't Hooper, did not ask for number 45, the chop suey.

The chow mein, number 34, was ordered by Alice.

Number 52, the prawn rice, was the request of Ms Farley and not, as he had just guessed, Bill Jackson.

Can you save the young lad's bacon by refreshing his memory as to which person ordered what?

WHY WERE THE BOY CHEESEMITE AND THE GIRL CHEESEMITE CRYING IN THE STILTON CHEESE?

Their love was in vein (in vain!)

	Farley	Goldsmith	Hooper	Innis	Jackson	Foo Young	Chop Suey	Chow Mein	Prawn Rice	Special	16	21	34	45	52
Alice															
Bill															
Charles															
Dora															
Eileen															
Foo Young															
Chop Suey															
Chow Mein															
Prawn Rice															
Special															
16															
21															
34															
45															
52															

First Name	Surname	Dish	Number
Alice			
Bill			
Charles			
Dora			
Eileen			

Flash Crash (??)

KEITH: Now, on Saturday Sportshow we take you back live to Ballybrakedown for the latest report on the Irish Grand Prix – over to *you*, Moray.

MORAY: And the excitement here is – *tremendous*. All sorts of things happening since you were last with us. Now there are only five cars left in the race and I want to tell you that:

Fire put young Chappell out of the race and fans of Max will be disappointed to hear that he didn't finish, after hitting a patch of oil in his Flash.

Clive drove the Streak and the Lightning caught fire.

Steve Quest was taken to hospital, though we are pleased to say he wasn't badly hurt, after losing the bend.

Morelli ran out of fuel and Phil Davies drove the Zoom.

Over to you, Keith, in the studio.

KEITH: I make that four cars out of the last five have each suffered a different disaster – so WHO WON?

MORAY: Sorry, Keith, can't hear you.

KEITH: Listeners, we seem to have lost the line to Ireland – so we'll have to ask you to tell us who won and what car he was driving.

WHERE DID THEY PUT THE MAN WHO SURVIVED BEING RUN OVER BY A STEAMROLLER?

In hospital, of course, in wards 5, 6, 7 and 8.

	Bennett	Chappell	Davies	Morelli	Quest	Flash	Jet	Lightning	Streak	Zoom	WINNER	Fire	Lost Bend	No Fuel	Oil Patch
Clive															
John															
Max															
Phil															
Steve															
Flash															
Jet															
Lightning															
Streak															
Zoom															
WINNER															
Fire															
Lost Bend															
No Fuel															
Oil Patch															

First Name	Surname	Car	Event
Clive			
John			
Max			
Phil			
Steve			

SOLUTION ON PAGE 177.

Daylight Robbery (???)

It was unfortunate for Constable Paynting that he was on traffic duty at the town roundabout just as a daring robbery took place along West Way. The escaping criminal headed in his direction and transferred the swag under his very nose to a van which the accomplice drove away.

It being a hot and sultry afternoon the policeman was beset with the problem of deciding whether to wave the traffic along, thus making a pleasant breeze waft around his face or keep completely still and so reduce the perspiration each little movement caused. So preoccupied was he that his later report to the superintendent is a model of confusion.

Nobody entered and left the roundabout by the same road.

The driver of the van, who wasn't Mr Wilkins, passed two exits before turning off, and that was not along West Way.

The lady driver of the Mini arrived at the roundabout along Knoyle View but did not exit along the High Street, where the sports car went.

The saloon came from Bradley Road and Mr Lomond from the High Street.

The estate driver left by the road Miss Hammett arrived along, which wasn't Long Lane.

Neither Mrs Green nor the lady in the sports car used Bradley Road at all but the driver of the Mini did.

Can you save the constable's career by quickly slipping him the names of the two criminals involved, the cars they used and the roads they arrived and left by?

A similar list of the other road users will help establish their innocence.

Rainbow.

	Mini	Van	Saloon	Sports	Estate	Approach — High St	Approach — Long Lane	Approach — Bradley Rd	Approach — Knoyle View	Approach — West Way	Exit — High St	Exit — Long Lane	Exit — Bradley Rd	Exit — Knoyle View	Exit — West Way
Mr Lomond															
Miss Hammett															
Mrs Green															
Mr Wilkins															
Miss Lever															
Approach — High St															
Long Lane															
Bradley Rd															
Knoyle View															
West Way															
Exit — High St						✕									
Long Lane							✕								
Bradley Rd								✕							
Knoyle View									✕						
West Way										✕					

Name	Car	Approach	Exit
Mr Lomond			
Miss Hammett			
Mrs Green			
Mr Wilkins			
Miss Lever			

SOLUTION ON PAGE 177.

HIGH ST

WEST WAY

LONG LANE

KNOYLE VIEW

BRADLEY ROAD

AMAZING MAZES

Threading a maze is a popular pastime which has deep roots in both our religious and leisure past. In these mazes, though, you are not simply asked to make your way from A to B, but to take part in a mental steeplechase which has a variety of hidden hurdles. In some, you won't know your Up from your Down until symbols are decoded; in others you will try to retrace the path taken by a drunken ant after it unwittingly wandered through a puddle of best bitter.

The Marsh Of Mynog (?)

There is very little crime in the forests of Mynog, mainly because the inhabitants are too small to get up to much and the fearsome marsh contains creatures nasty enough to frighten anything into being good.

Also, the Mynogians discovered long ago that a guilty person becomes so obsessed with their dark secret that they cannot concentrate on even simple tasks, such as counting 1, 2, 3, 1, 2, 3, 1 . . .

Which is why, when they have to have a trial in Mynog, the supposed criminal is made to go through the dreaded marsh by jumping from stepping stone to stepping stone in correct order, 1, 2, 3, 1 . . .

They are only just big enough to jump from a stone to one of its neighbours and as they jump off a stone it disappears below the soggy, squelchy surface never to be seen, or used, again.

The mathematical marsh monsters keep a keen eye out for anyone breaking the rules and if someone does, GULP! then a crime is avenged.

Only an innocent person will be able to concentrate and find the one path through to freedom – can you?

Always. Year always begins with Y and end always begins with E.

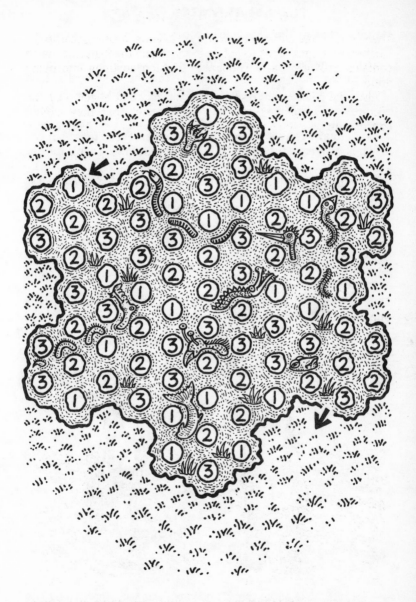

Sum Maze (?)

Maths lessons at the Dinglydell School For Worms are energetic events.

Each worm begins at the Start with a score of 10 and travels down the wormholes which connect the caverns. On arrival at each cavern the score is changed according to the number shown, if it is a *plus* the score increases by the number, if a *minus* then the score goes down.

On its journey a worm can visit each cavern several times but can only go down each tube once. It is too big to turn round in a tube as well and must go on to the next cavern.

As soon as the little chap reaches End the beetle in charge checks his score and off he goes for lunch.

If you were down there, what sort of score could you get?

Compare your effort to this worm's eye chart:

Below 20 : You're heading for the birds!

20 – 28 : Not good

29 – 38 : Not bad

39 – 48 : Now you are moving

over 48 : Excellent; go on to the next lesson – Black Holes And How To Dig Them.

HERE, WHY DO BEES HUM?

Bees hum because they don't know the words of the song.

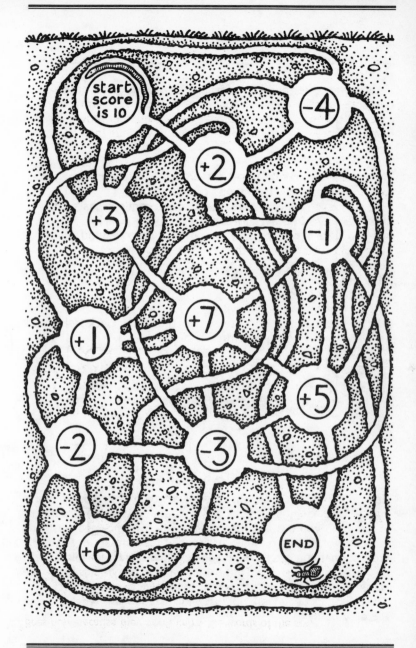

SOLUTION ON PAGE 182.

By the soap!

Clued Brick Cube (??)

Can you find the only route from start to end in this, the only
version of the iniquitous cube which doesn't move or fly apart just
at the time you are about to solve it? Each symbol has just one
meaning – Up, Down, Right, or Left and they are arranged on the
faces so that you can never, if you have the correct meaning, leave
the surfaces you can see. Thus it is clear from the symbols above the
starting square that neither circle nor triangle can mean left.

**Given that, can you work out just which sign means what and find
the only path?**

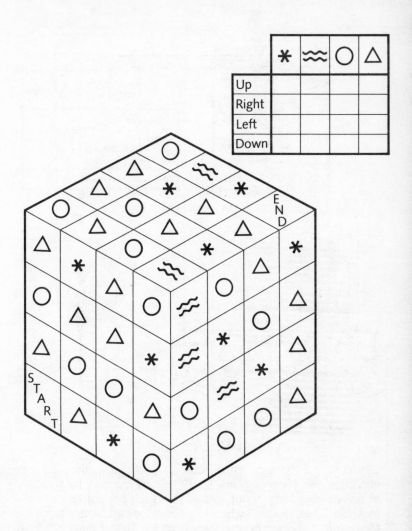

	*	≋	○	△
Up				
Right				
Left				
Down				

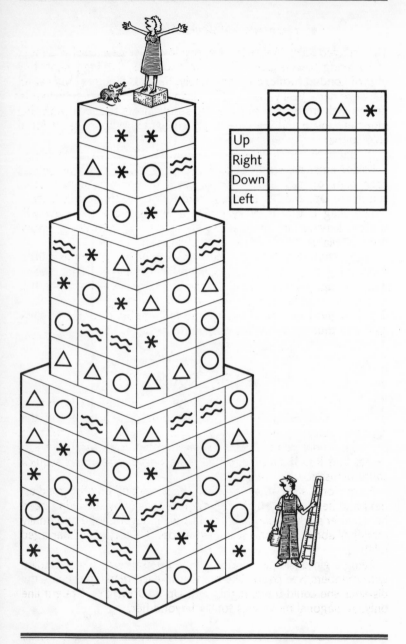

	≈	◯	△	✳
Up				
Right				
Down				
Left				

SOLUTION ON PAGE 178.

Devine Intervention (??)

The dreaded Killer Mouse has trapped lovely Dolores Devine on top of Tottering Towers (see left). Her thin screams, battling against the roar of London traffic, are, fortunately, heard by the only man who can save her – Wally the window cleaner. With his magnetic hands he can inch from pane to pane and so reach the top, deal with the monster mouse and save the lovely girl – before popping off for a chip supper.

If, that is, he can find the one safe route to the top of the building.

Killer Mouse has worked his wicked ways and painted a design on each pane of glass. Each symbol has a different meaning – one stands for Up, another Down, a third Right and the fourth Left.

The snag is that if Wally makes a wrong move the glass will shatter, leaving him clinging fiercely to thin air, and we all know how unreliable that is as a means of support.

Wally, though a wonder at scaling without scaffolding, is a little short on grey matter – he can't work out which symbol means what, though he has realized that he can stroll anywhere along the ledges which separate each section of the building.

Can you give him a mental hand and tell him the meaning of each sign and thus mark out the only route to the top?

Red Riding Route (??)

Just in case you've ever wondered why the wolf had so much time to get to Grannie's, ask after her rheumatism, bung her in the cupboard, dress up in the old lady's nightwear and put on a full face of make-up before the little girl came tripping up the path, we can reveal that Red Riding Hood had more on her plate than a quick sprint across town.

From Home she had to visit, first, the shops and buy the goodies, next find her way to, and through, the woods (why she didn't heed her mother's advice and take the bus we'll never know) and finally meander about until she stumbled across the cottage of her aged relative.

Being a girl of simple mind she armed herself with a map riddled with numbers (see over). The number in each rectangle shows the distance she could travel Right, Left, Up or Down in a straight line only. A diagonal move was totally beyond her.

The rectangle she landed on then gave her a fresh number of rectangles to move over for the next leg of her journey.

She must visit the shops and the woods in that order and then move on to Grannie's by landing on each of those rectangles at the end of a move.

She must never land on or pass over any of the named rectangles at any time other than when they are being visited in their correct sequence.

If she is ever going to catch that wolf napping she'll have to break the secret of the maze and mark the route to Grannie's.

Can you do that for her?

HOME 1	1	5	4	3	3	1	6
0	1	0	1	2	2	3	4
3	5	4	1	SHOPS 1	2	0	4
0	1	1	0	4	2	1	1
2	WOODS 1	5	2	0	3	3	3
0	0	2	1	3	4	3	6
2	3	2	2	4	1	0	GRANNIE'S

The Drunken Ant (?, ?? & ???)

Amateur naturalist Edwin Plotts did not have to travel far to enjoy his hobby for halfway up his garden path was a crack in the concrete which served as the front door to a large, multi-storey ants' nest.

It was Edwin's custom after Sunday lunch to encamp on the path surrounded by the paraphernalia of his science – a notebook, pencil, sunglasses and a pint of beer.

His speciality was *antics* – those apparently random movements of the species as they crossed and recrossed the path and flower

SOLUTION ON PAGE 179.

borders. He was convinced that if he selected one specimen and followed it for long enough, plotting its movements on squared paper, he would learn the secret of its navigation. Each square on his grid represented a small patch of ground and he entered an arrow to show the direction the ant was travelling in at the time.

The result of Plott's work is somewhat spoiled by two unscientific factors in his study – the records became so messy that squares the ant visited more than once were a useless splodge without discernible directions and the ant he selected had just passed through a puddle of beer spilt when the deckchair collapsed.

As he tries to recreate the ant's path he knows that each square with one arrow in is a square the ant visited once only. Those squares which contain a star are places the ant visited more than once. Also Edwin does recall that the ant always went straight on or turned right or turned left; it never turned round to leave a square the same way it entered by.

He has little hope of untangling this mess and finding the exact route the ant took but would like his records to show a possible path.

Can you find a way the ant could have made its journey?
Give yourself a bonus pat on the back if you can discover a path which takes the insect through the squares the least number of times.

1. SUNDAY 7th AUGUST (?)

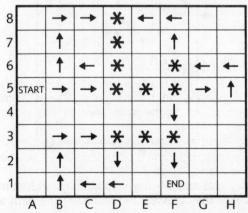

2. SUNDAY 14th AUGUST (?)

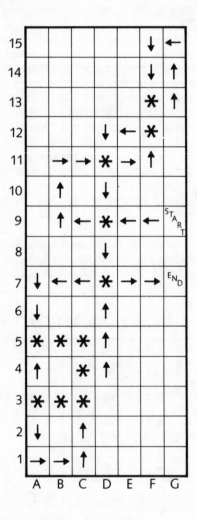

3. SUNDAY 21st AUGUST (??)

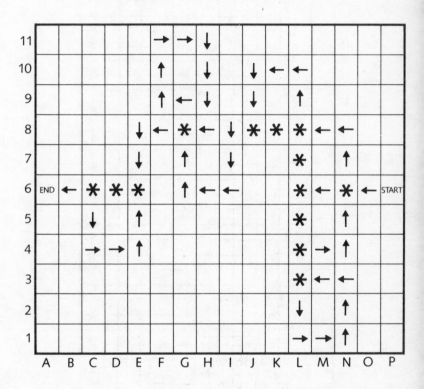

4. SUNDAY 28th AUGUST (???)

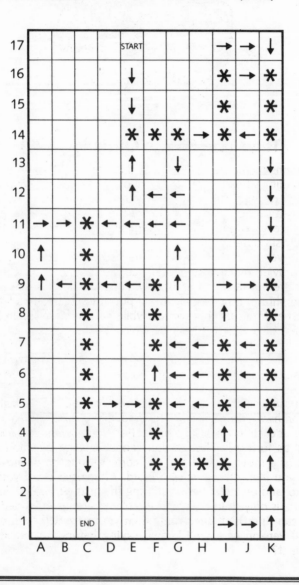

SOLUTION ON PAGE 181.

The Maze Phrase Of Philos (???)

Excavations by Sir Eustace Loffe at this site have thrown up fresh and startling theories on the life of the Ancient Greeks. The discovery of long, thin clay pots with narrow necks in what was probably a supermarket storeroom 30 feet below sea level has led Sir Eustace to suggest that the aqualung is much older than is generally supposed.

Controversial as this may be, the many clay tablets found at Philos provide much clearer evidence that many of our cherished sayings are not recorded accurately. For example, it is now known that the phrase 'It never rains but it pours' originated in a letter by Sossygenes to his mother written while he was travelling in Egypt. Referring to a wayward camel which would not submit to his control he wrote 'It never reins but it paws.'

The tablet shown overleaf is typical of the finds and shows one of the amusements the ancients enjoyed on the slopes below Olympus.

A phrase well known to them has been laid out on the slabs of a spiral pathway. Begin at START and move either three or five squares at each move to land on a letter. You may move backwards as well as forwards, though you cannot change direction in the middle of a move. If you find the correct sequence of moves the letters you land on will spell a word. After each word you must move to land on a star before starting the next word. Each letter in the spiral is only used once and the blanks are never landed on.

If you can find the hidden route then your path will spell out the original version of a well known saying before you reach END. What is it?

SOLUTION ON PAGE 182.

INITIATIVE TESTS

Can you spot patterns, make simple deductions or think laterally? If a straightforward connection doesn't immediately spring to mind, try taking a cockeyed look at the situation since, as you will no doubt soon discover, the author has a twisted, though fiendishly logical, view of life.

Missing Link (?)

Which of the four pictures, A, B, C, D, rightfully belongs in the empty space?

A

B

C

D

Ninewords (?)

In each grid opposite a nine-letter word has been rather carefully spread around. To find the word, first find the right place to start and then trace out a path from letter to letter by moving up, down, right, left or diagonally to the next square.

The words are all in common use and there is a clue to each should you need it.

SOLUTION ON PAGE 184.

1

A	M	A
L	R	M
A	D	E

On the break-
fast table.

2

S	E	L
P	C	E
E	O	T

Far-seeing.

3

N	B	D
O	A	M
T	N	I

Indoor sport.

4

L	I	C
E	U	I
S	D	O

Very tasty.

5

E	N	G
I	X	P
R	O	L

Going places.

6

S	E	L
S	E	N
S	I	O

Without
sound.

7

D	E	P
N	S	E
O	V	R

Get into debt.

8

Y	A	D
Y	S	R
E	E	T

It's in the
past.

9

C	I	A
T	R	C
A	B	O

Very agile.

SOLUTION ON PAGE 184.

Jekyll & Hyde? (?)

Two famous TV stars are on this 'box' today, though the picture is rather scrambled! Can you switch to the right channel and say who they are?

In The Picture (?)

One of the four pictures A, B, C, D, belongs in the empty space — can you work out which?

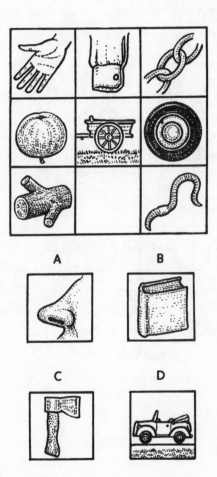

SOLUTION ON PAGE 184.

Fruit Salad (?)

Four different fruits, each a five-letter word, have been thoroughly mixed up in this bowl.

You could just list the letters and painfully make up the names of the four fruits but, thanks to the special power of our mixer, the parts have been very logically scattered.

Can you quickly sort out what has been done and so name the ingredients of this dish?

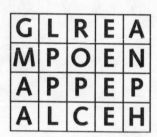

Switch Word (?)

One of the words in box B belongs in box A – which is it?

A	B

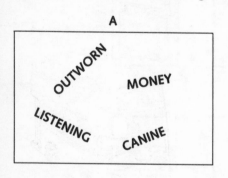
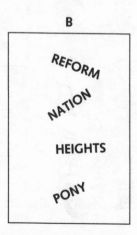

Time For The Bus (?)

What number should be on the bus which leaves the depot at 6.18?

Departs 4.36

Departs 3.24

Departs 5.20

Departs 2.14

Departs 7.42

Departs 6.18

SOLUTION ON PAGE 183.

Pick A Pic (?)

Which of the pictures, A, B, C, D, belongs in box number two?

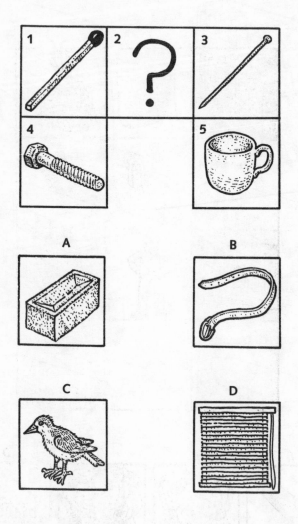

SOLUTION ON PAGE 183.

Links (?)

Which of the four pictures, A, B, C, D, fits into the empty space?

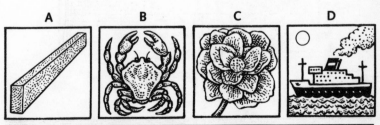

SOLUTION ON PAGE 183.

Missing Four (?)

It is probably obvious that C, F, L, M, are missing from this square, but where does each letter belong?

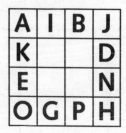

Number Please (?)

Which number belongs in the empty square?

1	1	2	1	2
2		4	5	3
1	4	3	2	1

Don't Touch (?)

What letter is needed to complete this square?

SOLUTIONS ON PAGES 183 AND 184.

Speech bubble: OI, WHERE CAN YOU BUY A NUCLEAR COMPUTER FROM?

A fission chip shop.

Meet The Dealer (? & ??)

Among the many unsung heroes of the real wild west is a shadowy figure known simply as 'the dealer'.

He was never the stuff of which films would be made; he didn't carry a gun, nurture a civil war grudge for 20 years or save Wyatt Earp's life. And he died, peacefully, with his boots *off* in a hotel for retired gentlefolk.

Yet he left behind a legacy of tales, some true, some mythical, which will outlast any gunfight at the Not-So-Bad Corral.

Part of the aura which surrounded him whenever he travelled the frontier trails was caused by his hands which were were exceptionally clean and well-tended for those largely unwashed times.

They needed to be, for he could look at a pack of cards once and, with a quick riffle, deal any hand or the complete pack in any order he chose.

It was his enjoyment to lay out a spread of cards on the green baize with one card turned over and challenge his onlookers to name the hidden card correctly, there always being some logic to the layout. Mostly he did this for amusement, such as in the Seattle Square, designed purely for children. On some he accepted wagers as to the name of the card and would earn many a comfortable night's lodging from his puzzled gold diggers.

Three of his more famous hands are shown on the next two pages. If you had been with Zeke at the Malemute Saloon, could you be sure of making a winning bet?

Seattle Square (?)

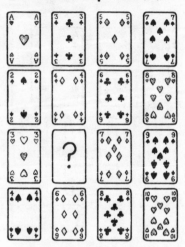

Denver Diamond (?)

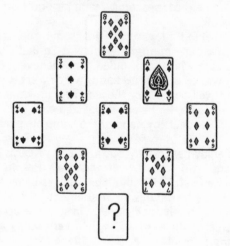

SOLUTIONS ON PAGE 183.

Toledo Triangle (??)

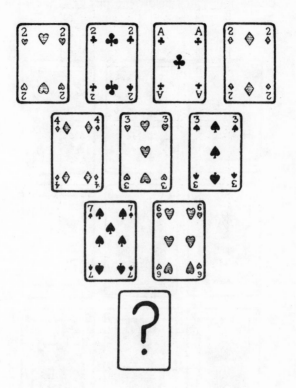

Get The Picture (??)

Just one of the four cards below the picture is the right one to complete it.
Which?

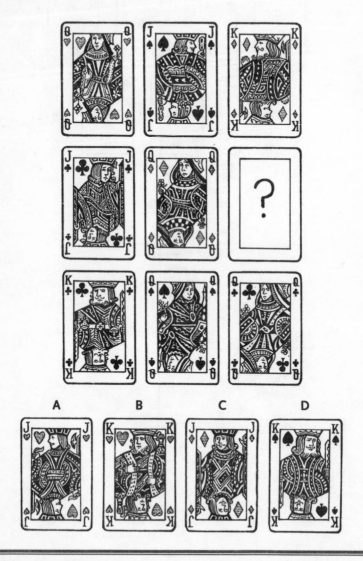

SOLUTION ON PAGE 183.

Cup Tied (??)

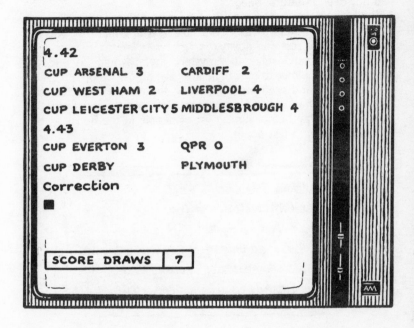

```
4.42
CUP ARSENAL 3        CARDIFF  2
CUP WEST HAM 2       LIVERPOOL 4
CUP LEICESTER CITY 5 MIDDLESBROUGH 4
4.43
CUP EVERTON 3        QPR O
CUP DERBY            PLYMOUTH
Correction
■
```

SCORE DRAWS	7

It was really too much for Bert when the operator of the teleprinter results service realized he had missed the goals off the last match and left the cursor blinking for what seemed an eternity.

It was even worse when the presenter of the programme cheerfully moved on to the horseracing results and left Bert with seven score draws and needing that one missing result to be a draw as well to win the jackpot he had dreamed of all his life.

Had he but known it, he could work out the result of that missing match from those on the screen above it – incredible as it may seem the scores are all logically determined.

Did Bert win the pools that week, or did he have to be satisfied with a smaller dividend?

SOLUTION ON PAGE 183.

Poetic Justice (??)

When the celebrated poet, Phineas Phearst, died at his country house it was fairly obvious to the local constable that his departure had not been a natural one.

The knife sticking out from the spot where Phineas normally kept his limp-bound notebook told Constable Paynting that here was his chance to show zeal and ability.

If only he could solve the mystery there would be enough feathers in his helmet to make him look like an ostrich on a bicycle.

The squad car's siren moaning along the distant drive told the officer that he had only a few moments to make the most of what little evidence lay before him: a list of people in the house at the time and Phearst's last poem.

> Mrs. Dora Phearst ~ wife
> Reggie Cornwallis ~ friend
> Alice ~ housekeeper
> Lord Peter da Quincy & his wife, Silvia
> Thomas ~ companion / chauffeur
> Morris Denham, publisher & his wife, Sadie

> Lewis Carroll had A
> Dream not once but every day.
> She saw what I
> Last left behind, slav
> Impressions o'er the sea.

The ink of the poem was still damp — he had written his final masterpiece with his murderer in the room, perhaps taking a twisted delight in granting him a last favour.

It must contain the identity of the murderer, if only Paynting could spot it.

He couldn't. Can you?

SOLUTION ON PAGE 184.

WHODUNNIT?

This chapter takes you back to the logical land of law and order and lets you play detective in a variety of visual and verbal situations. There are grids to fill in with the aim of eliminating suspects, photofit pictures to study for the one revealing clue, and tangled tales from dubious characters who cloud the issue with a cunning combination of truth and falsehood.

Pic Fit (?)

Five lots of witnesses have very kindly assisted police in their enquires and, helped by the station artist, have produced photofit pictures of four villains (Pictures 1 to 5). However, each witness has one detail wrong.

From their offerings the police have created five more possible pictures of the criminals (Pictures A to E).

In each case, which picture should the police publish as being the correct likeness?

ONE – Video shop break-in

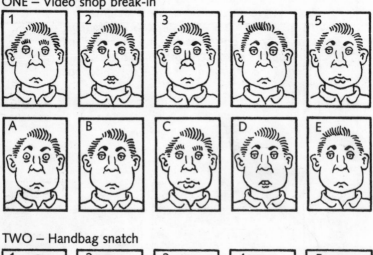

TWO – Handbag snatch

THREE – Shoplifting

1   2   3   4   5

A   B   C   D   E

FOUR – Vandalism

1   2   3   4   5

A   B   C   D   E

SOLUTIONS ON PAGE 185.

Victory On Paper (?)

As is often the case with local newspapers, the lavish interviews and photo sessions which give the participants the notion of a double page spread usually end up as a single picture and the wrong caption tucked somewhere between the fatstock prices and the council meeting reports.

Such was the case of the Hotel Europa's Grand Seaside Sports Tournament. Not a word was printed until the contestants had been reduced to the last four and then only a single picture of the tennis tournament with no caption. Which left the locals wondering what was going on. The two lines of text below the picture of the cricket contest shown the next week were a little more revealing but these two paled into insignificance when the final event, the golf contest, followed by the presentation of the trophy, was carefully captured for eternity *from behind*!

Could you just drop a line to the editor and tell him who won?

Brian Inglish receiving the first ball from Harry Scott while Colin Welsh keeps wicket and John Ireland waits for a catch.

SOLUTION ON PAGE 185.

The Long Shot (?)

When Alphonse Clotheade and Gaston Mugginge decided that only a duel could sort out their Gallic differences they chose modern weapons for the purpose. Early one morning they climbed a deserted nearby Alp and set off after each other with high-powered rifles equipped with telescopic sights and every modern hunting aid except radar, infra-red and silencers.

The only witness, Philip de Phluter, said later that he was talking to Gaston when the latter suddenly broke off, ran a few paces and raised his gun. Although Philip only heard one shot, Gaston fell dead nearly at his feet and later he found Alphonse, seriously wounded, on a small hillock two thousand metres away. When Alphonse was brought before the court on a charge of murder he pleaded guilty to manslaughter on the grounds of self-defence. His council, asked to explain this plea, stated that his client had fired after being fired upon and therefore could claim that he fired in self-defence.

It all depends on who fired first, so did Alphonse get away with the lesser charge or was he convicted of murder?

Open And Shut Case (?)

Using the new technology, Interpol have wired Scotland Yard that a spy carrying stolen documents is heading for Heathrow. They have managed to take a picture of him as he left Orly Airport.

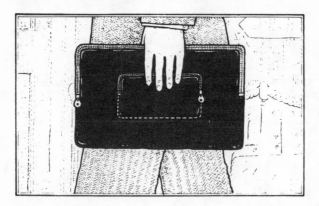

The information was rapidly passed to detectives at the airport but they were hampered by the number of similar men carrying similar cases all getting off the same plane.

Which man should the detectives arrest and search?

SOLUTION ON PAGE 185.

Cromwell's Revenge (?)

It was at least an hour before dawn on the morning of the Battle at Edgehill when a sentry on duty rushed to Cromwell's HQ and demanded to see that great soldier at once.

He was so insistent that Cromwell heard the noise and agreed that he would listen to his story.

'General', the man said, 'I beg you to stay away from the field today.'

Cromwell laughed out loud at this extraordinary request.

'Why?' he asked.

'I have just had a terrible dream,' said the lookout, 'in which I saw a royalist cannon explode in front of you. The blast knocked you from your horse and you were dragged right through the enemy lines to a horrible death. It must be a portent from God on High. I had to warn you.'

Looking grave, but inwardly feeling amused, Cromwell dismissed the man with his thanks and continued his preparations for battle.

When the day was nearly over he asked one of his aides to find out if the soldier had survived the battle as easily as he himself had.

On being told that the man had not been hurt at all, the leader of the parliamentary cavalry immediately ordered his execution.

Why? What had he done to deserve such a fate?

Truth Will Out (??)

'Don't look so down, my boy,' the gang's leader said as the cell door closed behind them. 'Alright, so they caught us with the jewels but there weren't any witnesses at the scene so we're sitting pretty.'

'How do you make that out?' another asked.

'Look. They do us for possession but unless the prosecution can make it clear exactly what happened at the raid, they can't convict us for it.'

'So what do we do?' asked the third.

'We just mix our statements up; all lies and truth together. That way they'll never work out which of us did which part of the raid. One of us though, is a bad liar, so he'll tell the truth all the time.

One can get away with a fib now and again, so he tells one true fact and one lie.'

'And the other one?'

'He lies both times. Come here. I've written down what we'll say:

ALF	I drove the van.
	Bert threw the brick.
BERT	Charlie threw the brick.
	Alf drove the van.
CHARLIE	Bert waved the gun around.
	I drove the van.

Now memorize it. You'll see tomorrow, boys...'

'... and in conclusion,' said the judge, 'despite your efforts at subterfuge, it is clear what part each of you played in this raid and I will now pass sentence.'

Can you, like the judge, work out just who did what?[1]

1. I promise not to make a habit of these footnotes, I know how useless they usually are, telling you to read REX V SUGDEN 1792 or something. But just in case you find these puzzles a little hard to get cracking on, look up the solution to this one (pages 185 to 186) which will go into the matter pretty fully. This should then make the rest child's play. OK? Just thought I'd mention it.

Caught Napping (??)

It is surprising, really, that Sluffy's gang ever tried another kidnapping. The last time they did it the parents of a particularly repellent offspring had sent them a ransom note demanding payment if they returned the child!

This latest effort went sadly wrong as well – if you are going to climb in through a third floor bedroom window it is no use having a ladder just long enough to smash the glass on the second floor.

Having mixed with the criminal fraternity for long enough, they too hope to get away with dissembling, so when making their statements one tells the truth both times, one lies both times and one tries one of each variety. Though, in fact, each did one of the actions leading to the arrest.

SOLUTION ON PAGES 185 TO 186.

MUGSY	I wrote the ransom note.
	Sudsy climbed in the window.
PATSY	Sudsy wrote the ransom note.
	I set the ladder up.
SUDSY	I climbed in the window.
	Patsy wrote the note.

Can you work out what kind of truth-teller/liar each one is and so discover who had what function in that failed attempt?

Double Trouble (??)

Slugger blamed Toddy for the disaster and Ugly blamed both of them. What should have happened was that one would ram the mail van, one would spray the driver with a gas which would release him from all further interest in the proceedings and the third would break the lock. Thereafter they would work together to transfer the packages to their getaway fork lift truck.

What actually happened was that the rammer hit the wrong end of the van, was sprayed with gas by mistake and the third wasted precious seconds battering away at an unlocked door.

Awaiting trial they were invited for frank, round the table discussions with the police and, as sometimes happens, one broke down and told the truth but the other two lied steadily and completely.

SLUGGER	Toddy rammed the van.
	Ugly tried to break the lock.
TODDY	Ugly sprayed the gas.
	I rammed the van.
UGLY	I rammed the van.
	Toddy sprayed the gas.

Just for the prison record, can you say who had which job?

Fraudulent Conversion (??)

It is no surprise to those of us who receive gas bills for one million pounds and a demand for £0.00 from the rates people that computer systems can be easily corrupted.

Fergus, Howard and Gerald had quite a business going when one of them copied the key to the computer room, another slipped in after hours and arranged for the machine to print cheques for them and the third went to the bank to cash them.

When caught they, like so many others, thought that false admissions of guilt might hide the real state of affairs, so in the two statements made by each, one told the truth both times, another gave one honest fact and one false and the third offered two untruths:

FERGUS   I copied the key.
Gerald changed the program.
GERALD   Howard had the key copied.
Fergus collected the money from the bank.
HOWARD   Fergus changed the program.
Gerald made the key.

Can you work out just who did what?

A coach driver's egg sandwich.

Lorry Load Of Lies (??)

The four crooks hauled in for questioning over the lorry hijack on the M4 near Newbury had learned, while picking their mothers' purses, to tell the truth as much as possible. So each of them makes two true remarks and tells one lie. They thought the net result would be confusion for the force and were surprised when three were allowed home and the fourth invited to stay until it suited a court to throw a party in his honour.

ARTHUR   I was in London that day.
                I know Charlie did it.
                Barry and Don are good mates, they always work
                    together.
BARRY   I didn't take the lorry, I was in Norwich.
                Don didn't do it.
                Arthur and Charlie are as thick as ...
                    well, thieves.
CHARLIE I was in Southampton.
                Arthur took the lorry.
                Arthur lies when he says I did it.
DON   I was in Liverpool the day of the hijack.
                Barry? – I've never met him.
                Alf didn't do it – he can't drive.

Can you work out who was arrested?

Don't Bank On It (??)

Yet another gang has tried to make a withdrawal from their local branch without having previously opened an account.

  When caught because their getaway bicycles were parked on yellow lines, they made the usual vain attempts to cloud the issue by making their statements a dense mixture of truth and falsehood, although each of them did do one of the actions described. One told the truth in both statements; one lied in both of his statements and the third gave one true fact and one lie.

                JOE   I cut the alarm.
                             Limey grabbed the cash.
            KLIVE I grabbed the case.
                             Joe guarded the staff.
            LIMEY I cut the alarm.
                             Joe grabbed the cash.

Can you help an overworked policeman fill in his report by working out what part was taken by each man in the bank raid?

SOLUTIONS ON PAGE 186.

By bovvercraft.

Shopping Around (??)

The three young ladies being interviewed about a shoplifting spree did not exactly help their case by telling less than the whole truth to the probation officer.

Fortunately, Mrs Jones was a good enough student of teenage nature to know that the defiant one actually spoke the truth all the time and that the other two made one true statement each and one false one.

> **KAREN** Helen passed the goods.
> Jenny created a diversion.
> **JENNY** Karen passed the goods.
> Yes, I created the diversion.
> **HELEN** I took the goods out of the shop.
> Jenny passed them over.

They had hoped, poor things, for their individual guilt to be hidden and took the 'you can't prove anything' attitude. But it collapsed into tears a few minutes later when the officer told them exactly who had done which of the three jobs in their combined raid.
Can you work it out, too?

SOLUTION ON PAGE 186.

Sweet Reason (??)

That welcome return to the old days when a policeman walked his beat has been particularly useful in Middlewich where Constable Potts maintains a friendly peace over the housing estate.

He knows his charges only too well, especially the children. So when little Elaine comes sobbing out the story of her bag of sweets being taken from her hand he knows he will need to have a word with Johnny and Marcus. He knows too, that one will lie completely and the other tell the truth half the time. His only problem is who will do what today.

'Well, young gents. What have you got to say for yourselves?'

Marcus spoke up first: 'Johnny snatched the bag. I ran off with it.'

Johnny came back quickly: 'I snatched the bag. Marcus didn't run off with it.'

Potts thought for a moment or two. This was a tricky one. He looked around and then called Sheila over. She's another one who has learned to tell the truth only half the time and lie solidly the other half.

'What did you see, Sheila?' Potts asked.

'Marcus took the bag. Johnny ran off with it.'

'Ah! Thank you little lady. I now know what happened.'

Do you?

Visiting Time (???)

As the November fog closed in around Baker Street, Holmes sat in the corner of his room smoking quietly.

Eventually the long silence was broken by the sound of an approaching hansom, some muffled footsteps, a knock at the door and the arrival of a visitor.

Holmes threw the stranger a swift glance.

'I would suggest,' said the great man, 'that you recover a calmer poise before embarking on your incredible story.'

'How did you know I was agitated, Holmes?' the guest asked, 'I thought I wore the mask pretty well.'

'You have a slight limp in the left leg, indicating that

SOLUTION ON PAGE 186.

you have walked round and round in small circles for some time. There is a marked indentation on the index finger of your right hand, showing that you have been writing under pressure and it is not usual for gentlemen venturing abroad of an evening to wear a nightcap.'

'Incredible, Holmes,' Watson murmured,' I didn't notice a thing.'

'Mr Holmes, we at the Butterwick Private Clinic need your help. There has been a most dreadful crime committed and we are anxious to have a speedy apprehension of the criminal before the popular press can smear our establishment.'

'The facts, if you please.'

'We have been concerned over the health of one of our more wealthy clients, Lord Sherborne, for some time and therefore keep a constant but discreet watch on his room. His condition gave no cause for alarm this evening and several visitors came and went. The nurse on duty knew some by name, or heard given names being used and deduced the professions of some who were un-known to her.'

He handed Holmes a sheet of paper (see over).

'As you can see, they seem respectable enough but it is clear that at some time in the evening one of them administered a poison to his Lordship, for we found him dead at ten this evening.'

'We can take it, I believe,' muttered Holmes, more to himself than anyone else, 'that this dose was slipped into his evening drink by someone who was, for a short time, alone in the room. To have done it before a witness would be risking too much.'

For a short while he studied the list, then grinned in triumph as he tossed the paper to his faithful friend.

'There you are, Watson. All the evidence you need to work out who killed Lord Sherborne. Though knowing you, you'll make up one of your wretched grids to help you sort out the facts. While you are at it, identify everyone else as well, won't you, my good fellow.'

Had you been in the doctor's shoes that night, would you need the five minutes or longer to say who killed his Lordship?

Messrs Davies, Finch, Marsh, Suggett. Christian names: Andrew, Cedric, James, Peter. Wives: Alison, Clare, Marie, Sonia.

8.40 pm ~ The surgeon went in with James and Mrs Davies.

8.50 pm ~ Sonia left, then Suggett, Andrew and Clare, the broker's wife, went in.

9.05 pm ~ The painter and Mr. Davies and Peter left, then the director's wife went in.

9.30 pm ~ James Finch left with his wife, Clare. Then Alison went in.

9.50 pm ~ The painter's wife and Marie left together.

The nurse is sure that each person only made one visit. She discovered Lord Sherborne dead at 10 pm.

	Davies	Finch	Marsh	Suggett	Andrew	Cedric	James	Peter	Alison	Clare	Marie	Sonia
Broker												
Director												
Painter												
Surgeon												
Andrew												
Cedric												
James												
Peter												
Alison												
Clare												
Marie												
Sonia												

SOLUTION ON PAGE 185.

Time	In	Out
8.40		✕
8.50		
9.05		
9.30		
9.50	✕	

Peach Surprise (???)

Holmes flagged down a passing hansom.

'The grill room of the Hotel Metropole and step on it,' he ordered, as he bundled Watson into the cab.

In the restaurant, Holmes' first glance took in the four frightened diners huddled in a corner, a constable swinging a nonchalant truncheon in front of them. At a side table a seated figure was slumped into the remains of a peach surprise. Inspector Tew of the Yard came bustling over.

'Ah, Holmes. Glad you could make it. Nasty business.'
'Ah, Tew,' said Sherlock.
'Bless you' said Watson, automatically. A withering look shot from under Holmes' beetling brows.
'Tell me all about it, Tew.'
'Five men booked in for dinner, sat at that table there. During the sweet course one slumps forward dead. Poison, and a quick one at that. Those four,' he indicated with a nod of the head, 'won't say a word – too frightened or too guilty.'
'Nothing to go on from the staff?' asked Holmes.
'Yes, though it doesn't make much sense to me yet.

The waiter has lost his order pad but recalls some of the details of what he served and he heard some names being thrown about while he was at the table.

'1. Each man had a different main course and sweet.

'2. Carter sat between Phil and Dent, who ate the trout.

'3. Sid Woodward did not order pork or steak and sat on the right of Charles who ordered the trifle.

'4. Hunter, who did not ask for steak or duck, ordered the fresh fruit and sat on the left of Phil who asked for cheese.

'5. The man who ate the steak also had the ice cream and sat on the right of the man who ordered pork, who was not Eric or Hunter.'

Without a word, Holmes strode to the table, stared at it for a few moments, turned to the inspector and, to his astonishment, said, 'This man was killed by the person sitting on his left who slipped the poison into his dish at a moment when the others were distracted by the cabaret, probably the can-can.'

'Incredible, Holmes!' Watson cried.

'A trivial case,' Sherlock muttered. 'And within your capabilities, my good doctor. Just give the officer the details of who is whom, sat where, ate what and, in particular, the name of the murderer.'

'I would do it like a shot, Holmes,' Watson mumbled. 'But I haven't eaten since lunch and they serve an uncommonly good steak here.'

For once, Holmes must provide the answers himself. Can you match his prowess and work out just who did it?

	Bert	Charles	Eric	Phil	Sid	Duck	Game pie	Pork chop	Steak	Trout	Cheese	Fresh fruit	Ice cream	Peach surprise	Trifle
Carter															
Dent															
England															
Hunter															
Woodward															
Duck															
Game pie															
Pork chop															
Steak															
Trout															
Cheese															
Fresh fruit															
Ice cream															
Peach surprise															
Trifle															

CARTER

?

Spear Murder (???)

Holmes' eyes wandered around the room, then alighted on the body of Lord Tayble which was resting quietly on the floor with three African spears protruding from the waistcoat.

'I think they came from that stand by the fireplace,' ventured Watson.

'Quite correct, my good doctor. And that report we have just received from young Ern, the grocery boy, settles the case as to who killed his Lordship earlier today.'

'Does it, Holmes? I don't see how.'

'Think, Watson. Upon receiving no answer to his knock, he entered the hall and deposited his box upon the hall table, being too lazy to do as he should and go round the back to the tradesman's entrance. He assures us the hall was empty . . .'

'Ah! and since we have established that at the time of the murder there was just one person in each room, aside from the victim, naturally, then . . .'

'There must have been someone in the library with Lord Tayble. And yet, doubtless through fear of in-criminating someone close, if not themselves, each person has claimed to be in a room different from the one they actually occupied at the relevant time.'

'Yes, Holmes. I have constructed a sketch of the situation as they would have us see it.' (See right)

'I don't see that it helps us much, there are so many places where each could have been.'

'Not if you consider the facts in conjunction with some splendidly vague and innocent-seeming questions which I have put to some of those present. It is then a simple matter to determine just who was where. Come, Watson, consider them again:

'Tara Lotte could hear a man singing and playing the piano in the room next to hers – and there is only one instrument in the house.

'The maid said that both the doors of the room she was in were shut.

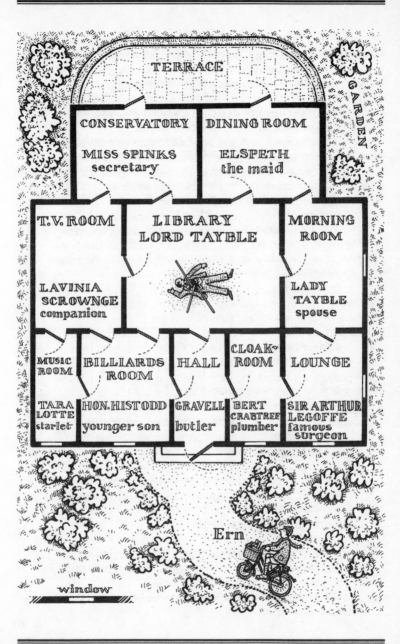

'Crabtree, the plumber, admitted that he would have to pass through two doors to get from the room he claimed to be in to the one he really occupied.

'Lavinia states that only one of the three doors leading from the room she was in was shut — that was the door to the library. From the rustling of clothes through the two open doors she is sure that a woman was in each of those adjacent rooms.

'Lady Tayble, who says she saw and was seen by the boy Ern, occupied a room adjacent to the one she claimed to be in.

'Sir Arthur Legoffe remained in the front part of the house and Miss Spinks was aware of the Hon Histodd in the room next to hers.

'Gravell, the butler, admits to being in the billiard room helping himself to cigars.'

'And that clears the whole mystery up? I don't see how.'

'Of course it does, my good fellow. It is so trivial that I shall practise my violin while you work out who was in the library and so committed the foul deed.'

As always, the poor Doctor is left to sort out just who was where and who used his Lordship as a spear holder.
Can you give him a hand, please, and slip him the answer before Holmes breaks a string?

	Conservatory	Dining room	TV room	Library	Morning room	Music room	Billiard room	Hall	Cloakroom	Lounge
Miss Spinks	X							X		
Elspeth the maid		X						X		
Gravell the butler								X		
Lady Tayble					X			X		
Sir Arthur Legoffe								X		X
Tara Lotte						X		X		
Hon Histodd							X	X		
Bert Crabtree								X	X	
Lavinia Scrownge			X					X		

TEAM GAMES

In this chapter you are invited to gather together a company of lively souls and pit your wits against each other as you seek the elusive answer to a baffling story. Here your clues will come from what the team thinks and what questions are asked.

Solving puzzles is, for the most part, a very solitary occupation. A railway compartment of crossword addicts looks like the annual convention of the KGB; there is no free swapping of answers and comradely chaff about missed anagrams, only eight stiff newspapers held up like fencing masks before eight grim faces, who may as well be on eight different planets.

Team Games are the complete opposite. So gather the family or friends around you, take turns to be question master, and try to fathom the strange truths behind these weird tales. For each round, one person reads the story to the rest whose task is then to explain what has happened. The reader will, of course, look up the answer. Then anyone in the group can ask a question which must be capable of being answered by a simple 'yes' or 'no'. The object is not just to find a reasonable answer to the facts given in the story but to get to the particular answer given in this book. Though the whole thing may seem impossible, improbable and impracticable, once the questions start flying, you will ferret out the solution, with tremendous fun during the hunt.

For the next round the chairperson can be whoever gave the correct solution to the last puzzle or you may prefer to give each member of your group a turn at being in charge.

Late Lamented (?)

Spare a thought for Fred and Freda,
Lying dead upon the floor.
Broken glass 'midst scattered pebbles
And a cloth half through the door.
Who were Fred and Freda?

Fur Enough (?)

A woman is walking slowly up and down at one of the larger of London's railway stations. She stops, searches her handbag and puts a coin in a slot.

She frowns, searches for another coin and is about to put that in the slot when she pauses, takes off her expensive fur coat, folds it neatly over one arm and then deposits the coin.

She grunts in disgust and quickly walks away.
What was she doing?

SOLUTIONS ON PAGE 187.

A Ferry Close Affair (?)

The man carrying the suitcase came round the corner of the warehouse at a fairly leisurely pace but immediately broke into a frantic run when he saw the ferry, fully laden, a few feet from the jetty ramp. With some considerable skill the man wheeled his arm and let go of the case at just the right instant for it to describe a beautiful arc and land with a soft thud on the car deck of the ferry. Taking a few steps back and then putting in a sprint which would have impressed Daley Thompson, the man threw himself into the air and over the water and just managed to scramble aboard the lowered end of the vessel.

The look of triumph on his face quickly turned to despair as the first mate helped him to his feet with a few words of welcome.

What did the officer say to cause such a change of mood?

The Death Call (??)

The police were quite sure; death had been due to accidental, if somewhat bizarre, circumstances.

They had been called to the telephone box by one of their associates from the river police who had noticed something odd by the bridge. Upon investigation the officers had found a man slumped in the box dying from loss of blood. Two panes of glass on either side of the box were smashed and the telephone hung from its cord.

Who was the man and how did he so tragically meet his end?

Short Stop (??)

Another true story from my days – and nights – working at a local filling station. A car pulled in one day and the driver asked for two gallons of petrol, which I served him. We then spent some time carefully searching the car before, with a sigh, he climbed back into the driving seat and moved off. As he drove away, he called out, 'I didn't really want the petrol, you know.'

Can you work out what had happened and what we were up to?

SOLUTIONS ON PAGES 188 AND 189.

WHAT HAS 8 WHEELS AND FLIES ?

Two council dustcarts.

Knees Down (??)

There they are — eleven grown men, in a straight line, crawling on hands and knees across a school playground.
What on earth are they up — or rather down — to?

Bus Stop (??)

(Another true tale — this time from the Midlands)

When the young man climbed the stairs and took his seat near the rear of the double decker waiting at Birmingham Bus Station, he saw only one other passenger — an elderly man seated near the front.

Eventually the bus left the station and headed on its way towards Worcester. Later still, the conductor came up, collected the fare from the young man and moved forward down the bus. He tapped the elderly passenger on the shoulder and, oddly, an argument quickly developed.

It ended with the bus stopping between two stops and the man being put off, still clutching his ticket.
Is there a rational explanation for the conductor's apparently harsh conduct?

The House Call (??)

When Henry Kingsbury entered the house he paused, cursing quietly in the darkness, and then fumbled his way to the lounge. He turned on the light and moved towards the fireplace where the dying embers gave only a hint of warmth. Suddenly he threw his arms upwards and leaned on the chimney breast, hands high against the wall.

He stayed like that for some seconds and then collapsed on the floor in hysterics.
Can you explain this strange conduct?

SOLUTIONS ON PAGES 187, 188 and 189.

Field Find (??)

When Vincent Dewhurst takes up a hobby, he does so thoroughly. To him, country walking means far more than a train ride from his inner city flat and a stroll round some country station's coal and livestock store. Which is why he equipped himself with thick alpine socks, stout boots, hooded anorak, field glasses and the *Readers' Digest Bedside Book of Furry Friends*.

When he returns to his concrete forest after each expedition his notebook is filled with details of all he has seen. One entry, though, puzzles him.

On the edge of Chormley Wood, close by the new housing estate, he had passed through a gate and his keen eyes had noticed several pieces of coal – and a carrot.

How they came to be there is something he cannot explain – can you?

First – And Last – Order (??)

It was unusual for the regulars of the Plucked Pheasant to hear such words but one night a stranger did enter the four ale bar and ask for a glass of water. To their further astonishment the barman reached under the bar, picked up a shotgun and pointed it at the man.

The man then thanked him and walked, smiling, into the autumn night.

Later that night the puzzled locals could not explain the events to their wives, but can you?

Little Boy Blue (??)

The policeman on traffic duty near the tower block took only a quick, automatic, mental note of the small boy who stamped angrily down the front steps and off along the road. He took a little more interest when the lad came round the block behind him and began to make a second lap of the square, still with his head down and lower lip jutting.

After three more laps the officer took advantage of a lull in the traffic to stop the boy, kneel down beside him and ask what he was doing.

What explanation did the boy give for his somewhat unusual behaviour?

SOLUTIONS ON PAGES 187 AND 189.

Domestic Tiff (??)

It is amazing how often a trivial, innocent act can set off such a row in the home that it seems only the United Nations can solve the resultant crisis. Like the wife who inadvertently puts one of her husband's socks in the top drawer and the other in the second. He, of course, always wants that very pair of leg warmers on the day he has an important meeting and is late for the train.

For Mr & Mrs Platt their version of World War Three started one night with this simple scene...

Mrs Platt is kneeling on the floor. In front of her is a long piece of wire and by her side a pile of tiny electrical components such as are used in computers. She is already very angry indeed. Her husband is also in the room, at present unaware of the bomb that is about to burst. He is speaking on the telephone.
Just why is the good lady so angry?

The Riddle Of The Crying Man (???)

Two men are lying by a hedge near a van parked by the side of a country road. One of the men is dead, the other is crying quietly with an occasional, near hysterical, half sob – half laugh. Both men are in uniform but the uniforms are not the same.
Who are the two men and how did they come to be in that situation?

Unlucky Thirteen (???)

The rush hour in Los Angeles is never an experience to enjoy. The buses, though obeying traffic regulations, always look like motorized porcupines with bits of people and packages sticking out in all directions.

On Friday 13 February, number 13, the 17.13 from the City Library made its last downtown stop before hitting the freeway and heading for the suburbs.

As usual the cry went up: 'Hey bud, shift along the bus. Twelve standing only'.

'C'mon, Mac, move it, will ya?'

What made this day different from all the rest was that, just before the doors closed an extra passenger squeezed his way aboard and the bus moved off with its fatal cargo – 13 standing passengers.

SOLUTIONS ON PAGE 187.

An argument soon developed, involving the extra passenger, the other legal standees and the man in charge of the bus. The argument became rapidly acrimonious and he stopped collecting fares and tried to persuade the gatecrasher to jump back off, while the bus was still travelling slowly. Tempers rose between the two men, a fight developed and the 13th passenger fell dead from a blow to the head.

The man was tried on a charge of murder one, found guilty and sentenced to death in the electric chair.

His appeal failed and eventually he was taken from Death Row, given the last rites and strapped into the chair. At a nod from the governor the switch was thrown. Nothing happened. The chair was checked but found to be in full working order. Again the ritual was repeated and the switch thrown. Still nothing happened.

Eventually the guilty party was taken to another prison and again taken through the awful procedure of being affixed to the chair and the switch pulled. Still nothing happened – he even managed a weak smile.

Eventually, the authorities ran out of chairs and the man was paroled, having been considered to have suffered enough for his crime.

Just what was it that saved the man?

Dash It (???)

It was a very hot summer's evening as Peter Irvin strolled along the quiet avenue in the residential estate just north of Middle Yammering. He appeared to have little on his mind when he stopped, looked first puzzled and then alarmed.

He listened intently, head to one side, his left ear a dish aerial seeking the source of some distant message. Then he was off, dashing across the road, narrowly avoiding a collision with a very large boy on a very small BMX, vaulting a garden wall and rushing up the rose-bordered path of a suburban semi.

Without hesitation he attacked the front door and burst in – to be confronted with a very surprised and irate lady who, with each passing second, was becoming as explosive as a match in a firework factory.

Can you give some rational explanation for the man's behaviour which will mollify the lady?

SOLUTIONS ON PAGES 187 AND 188.

A Moving Experience (???)

A young man is drawing. Slowly, he leans forward then stops drawing. He runs a few steps and starts drawing again.

Once more he leans forward then stops drawing and runs forward again.

He keeps doing this for a while until eventually he stands still.
What is he doing?

Down – And Out (???)

It is Saturday morning in the High Street. A man is lying down in the road between two stationary cars.
What is he doing there?

Stringing You Along (???)

(This one is also true – on my honour!)

I was working late one Sunday night at a local filling station when a car pulled in. Despite the dreadful weather the side windows were down. Inside were a very bedraggled couple. He was in the driving seat with a length of string going across his body and out of the window. His wife, in the front passenger seat, was clutching the end of the string in one hand, and, in the other, the end of another piece of string which disappeared out of her window.

Unfortunately, I was unable to help them.
What was their problem, and what had they done about it?

Ah – Agh! (???)

Two men were sitting at a table. For 2 hours and 43 minutes there had been complete silence. Quite suddenly one of the men stood up with a yell of triumph – which quickly turned into a shriek of agony.
What were the men doing – and what happened to one of them?

SOLUTIONS ON PAGES 188 AND 189.

CARDBOARD
AND
COUNTERS

Before television took over the sitting room and stifled all activity, mechanical puzzles and games delighted many generations of children and adults. Here is your chance to make, and play with, puzzles which are Victorian in style but new in concept. Indeed, puzzles like Reversit and Square Around have never appeared in a book before, so you have an opportunity to achieve a World's First with the best solution.

This chapter forms the basis for many evenings of pleasure and creative entertainment.

Coin Op (?)

The meter needle on this strange coin op is hovering dangerously near *empty*. To save the washing from disappearing down the waste pipe it must quickly be fed with one each of the coins from 1p to 50p. But the coins must go in the compartments in such a way that adjacent boxes must not have coins with adjacent values. In other words the 2p must not be next door (in the same row and column) to the 1p or the 5p and the 20p must not be next to the 10p or 50p and so on.

To help avert the disaster one coin, the 5p, is already in place and the 20p will be to the left of the 1p.

Hurry now! Can you find the five coins and pop them into place?

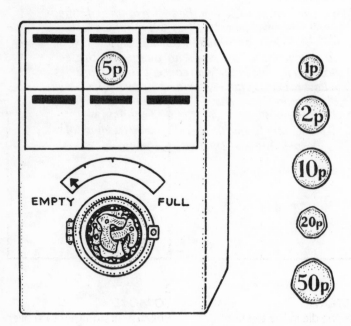

High Die Hi! (?)

All you need for this rather novel little game is a pencil and a standard die. With luck you will have a die which just about fills one of the squares on the board; if not, it might be an idea to draw a board to fit whatever die you managed to find underneath the settee!

The idea, naturally, is to roll the die in such a way that you end up with the highest score you can.

Our score of 28 is not very good so you might like to try and beat it on the board on page 133.

For fun with family and friends make up your own grid, one for each player, place each die the same way up at the start and set your digital watch to an agreed alarm time and away you go. Whoever has the highest score when the watch bleeps is the winner.

On your own at the moment? There are two more boards on page 134 for you to pit your wits against.

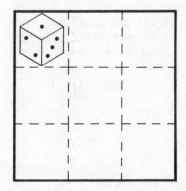

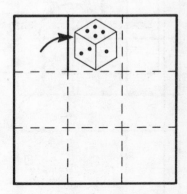

1
TO START
Place the die in the top left corner with the 1 spot on top, the 2 spot facing towards you and the 3 spot on the right.

2
TO MOVE
Roll the die a quarter turn over a bottom edge so that it moves into an adjacent square. Then draw in the line the die has just rolled over.

SOLUTION ON PAGE 436

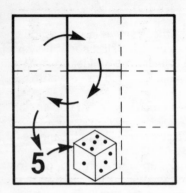

3
FILLING A BOX
After several rolls you will eventually roll and draw a line which completes a box (just as in the children's game called *Boxes*.) As a box is completed it scores points. The number is whatever is on top of the die at that move and the score is put in the box.

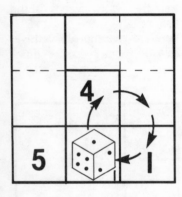

4
TWO BOXES FILLED AT THE SAME TIME
Drawing a line may complete two boxes. Put the top die number into *both* boxes. (Lift the die carefully and be sure to replace it without twisting it round.)

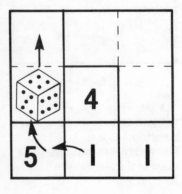

5
SPECIAL RULE
You cannot roll the die over a line which is already drawn in unless you have no other choice. Here, the die must be rolled upwards.

SOLUTION ON PAGE 150

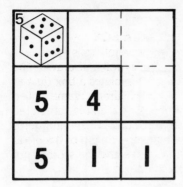

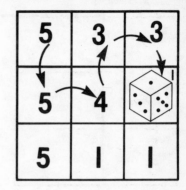

6
FREE ROLL
In this position you can roll to the right or down as both lines are already drawn.

7
THE END
When all the boxes have been completed add up the numbers to get your total score. Here it is 28.

See how many points you can score on this board and the ones on the following page.

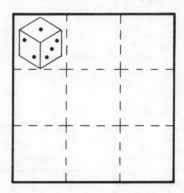

SOLUTION ON PAGE 190.

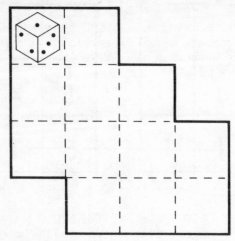

Target Score : 60 or more.

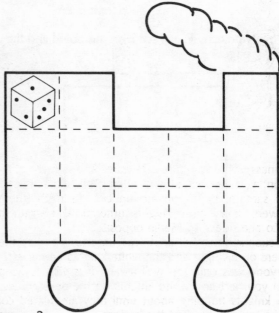

Top Score ...?

SOLUTION ON PAGE 190.

Over Knight Stop (?)

Never mind the Round Table at Winchester; dismiss it as nothing more than a medieval mistake. Thanks to the excavations at the bottom of his Somerset garden, Walter Wall has unearthed the original genuine table.

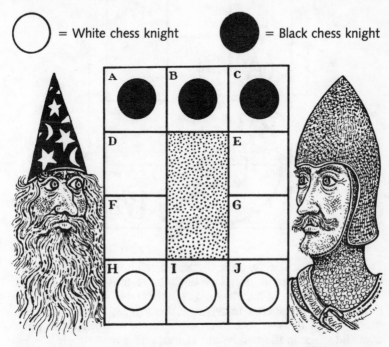

○ = White chess knight   ● = Black chess knight

The roundness of the structure is revealed as a figment of Malory's imagination; as is the vast array of titled gents, each dressed, like a millionaire sardine, in his private tin can. In truth, the weekly meetings were lucky if all six knights turned up and Arthur sat, very carefully, to one side with Merlin opposite.

To the superstitious Arthur it was unfortunate that the black knights were on his right and the white knights on his left.

As everyone was only too well aware, it is vital to keep black knights on your left and white knights on the dexter side. Which means six knights hopping about until they are seated correctly, white at the top and black at the bottom.

Naturally they will hop like knights – two places in one direction and one at right angles as if they were playing chess.

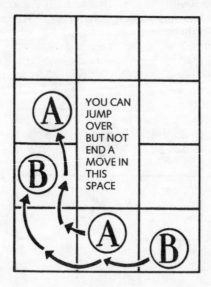

These knights are pretty agile chaps and will hop merrily over each other to land in an empty place but they cannot land on another knight – the crash of metal would be unbearable and it would take more than a tin opener to separate them again. One knight can make several hops in succession in the same move. He can jump over the space in the middle but cannot end a move there.

Merlin is already becoming impatient and is likely to break out at any moment in a rash of spells so, quick! Can you cast your own counters on the board and switch them over in the fewest number of moves?

Change In the Weather (?)

Sales at the Take-Me-Home Novelty Shoppe on Maricoombe seafront were down. True, there was a queue stretching from the front door right down to the beach, but that was for the ET Rock Arcade two doors along.

SOLUTION ON PAGE 189.

As Gus Johnson stared glumly at the piled up stock he could only blame himself for going off to the races on the one day when all the sales reps called round.

His assistant had not chosen very wisely. What demand could there be in a northern resort for a floppy hat which said 'Kiss Me Quick' in Japanese? Who was likely to buy suntan lotion in a ten gallon drum? And as for the puzzle book – was there another one in the country where the 'Spot The Difference' problem had only *one* picture?

Gus shook his head sadly, which was a mistake because it brought into view the plastic weather houses, all 200 of them. Who else but his Jim could claim there was a sure-fire winner here when the happy face said WET and the sad face DRY?

Still, there was hope for this item as the letters were written on plastic tiles set in a plastic tray and, though they could not be lifted off, they could slide around within the ten squares and so it might be possible to change the words over. (See picture on page 138.)

Gus sighed, he had tried and eventually succeeded, but converting all the stock would be a long job. If only he could find the quickest way of doing it it might at least make the task bearable.

To try to find the answer he has copied the grid, numbered the squares and made six counters from card for the letters.

His first moves are:

2 to 7;   1 to 6;   7 to 1.

Can you give him a hand by carrying on from there and finding out how to swap the words over?

To test your seaside skill here's how you can rate your effort:

Number of Moves	Rating
Over 45	Windy!
41 – 45	Dull with fog patches.
36 – 40	Fair.
31 – 35	Bright intervals.
26 – 30	Good – a few scattered showers.
Under 26	Excellent prospects.

SOLUTION ON PAGE 189.

Reversit (??)

Puzzlers of the world, unite! We are an endangered species. This deplorable modern fad of keeping fit is in danger of wiping us out.

Just as we settle into a deep armchair with the feet on the mantelpiece and the mouth sucking a thoughtful pencil, in itself sufficient exercise for any right thinking person, a mass of joggers passes the window urging us, with twisted facial gestures, to get up, out and join them.

We refuse, of course. But we are left with that nagging feeling that perhaps we should go along with the tide of opinion.

It is fortunate that doctors advise beginners to stop the activity as soon as the breath becomes short which in our case means we can legally give up while still struggling into the raincoat and woolly socks.

As we collapse again into that armchair the feeling of guilt remains. If only there were some activity which looks physical enough to delude the passer-by but which is more to our intellectual taste.

Reversit is just that – a hobby puzzle so physically hard and mentally mindbending that it could serve all your needs right through to the next century.

It is also your chance to achieve a world first, no one has yet discovered the best solutions to the puzzles, though we assure you that, tough as you may find the going, all can be solved and probably in less than 60 moves.

First, the physical part. You will need nineteen reversible counters, perhaps you have the game Othello or its ancestor, Reversi. If not, you could use nineteen coins and have 'heads' and 'tails' instead of colours. In emergency, and be sure to get your doctor to check you over before attempting this, you could glue black and white draughtsmen together to make attractive double-sided counters.

If your counters are of suitable size, you could play on the board shown here, which is a miniaturized Solitaire frame; otherwise mark out your own version on card or wood, making sure the squares take whatever size counter you are using.

The basic idea is to place all the pieces white side uppermost and leave just one square empty. In these puzzles we use C3 but you can try other squares. On each turn one counter can move like a knight in chess and land in the one empty square on the board. As it lands, *it is turned over* to show the opposite colour. (See the illustrations on the following page.)

A4, D1, E4 or D5 can move into the empty square.

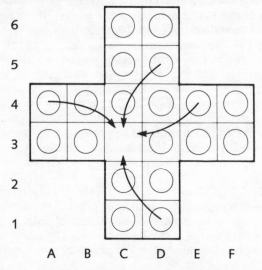

Move: D5 to C3. The counter is turned over as it is moved.

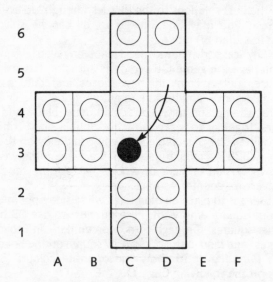

After the move you make 'captures' as in Reversi. Any counters lying in a straight line between the one which hasjust been moved and another of the same colour are turned over. The straight lines are horizontal or vertical only, not diagonal.

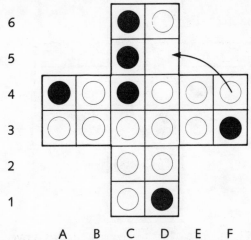

Counters at D4, D3 and D2 are trapped between the blacks at D5 and D1 and are turned over to black.

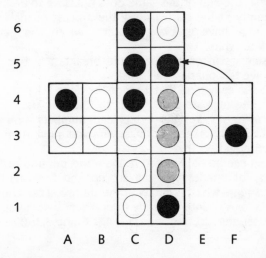

The black counter at C1 has moved to D3. The black counters at B3, C3, D2 and E3 are all captured and turned over to show white.

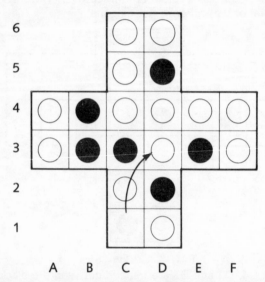

The idea is to end up with all the counters the other side up. The empty square at the end of the game does not have to be the one which was empty at the start. During the process of making the change you may have to make captures which change black counters back to white.

Give yourself a slap on the back and breakfast in bed if you manage to solve this puzzle at all!

You may feel in early trials that it cannot be done but rest assured it is possible. The ultimate challenge is to find out just how few moves you need to take; the letters and numbers around the diagram give a grid reference for the square you move from which can be written down.

More benefit can be obtained from the effort put into making it by the variety of puzzles you can set up and try. Apart from changing the square which is empty at the start, you can choose to have 0, 1, 2, 3, or 4 counters already turned over before you begin moving. The counters to turn are D1, F4, C6 and A3. (See pages 143 and144.)

Starting Positions

1

2

Starting Positions

3

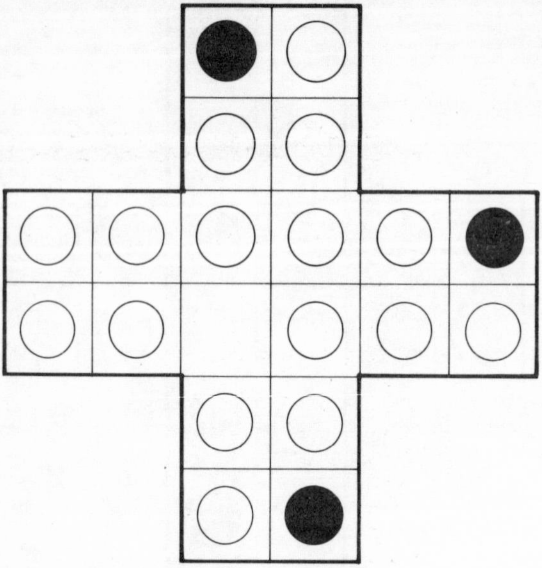

4

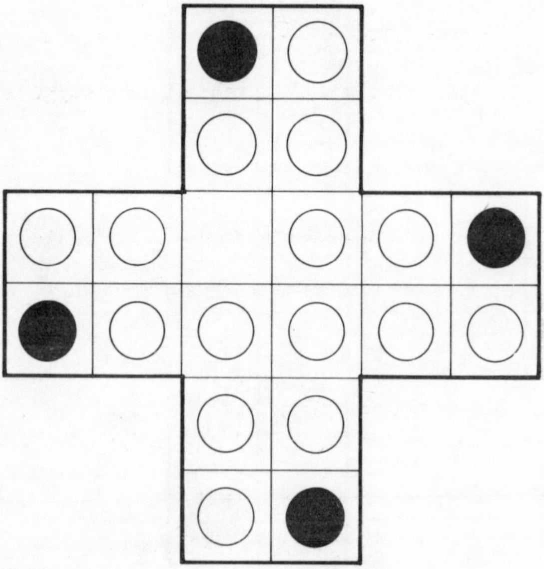

Since this is a genuine new puzzle with no past history we will not be offering any solutions here, thus giving you that real chance to climb a puzzler's Everest without leaving the comfort of your central-heatingside.

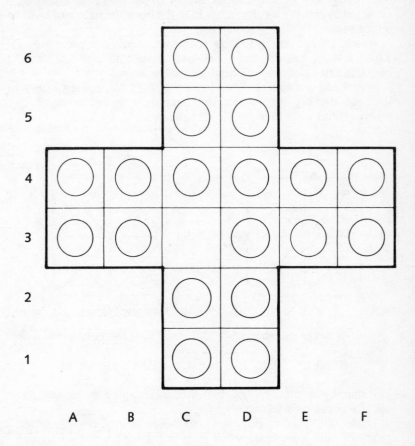

Queens High (??)

From the court of Ali Tel comes that old, old story. This Prince has 64 wives, a palace which in summer has a river at the bottom of the garden and in winter a garden at the bottom of the river, 2 very plain daughters and an eternal stream of would-be sons-in-law attracted by father's wealth rather than the beautiful nature of both princesses.

True to form, these unsuitable suitors are required to prove their worth and Ali has devised a two-part scheme to weed out the hopeless cases first and the brighter sparks second.

In part one the applicant had to arrange 8 of Ali's queens within the decorated courtyard (ignoring the numbers) in such a way that no two ladies were in the same straight line.

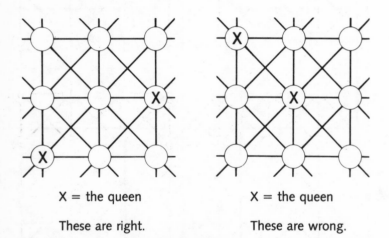

X = the queen   X = the queen

These are right.   These are wrong.

You might like to collect together 8 counters and a chessboard to see if you can pass the first hurdle.

Those who failed to do this within the passing of one thousand grains of sand from the celestial glass to the copper pot – roughly five minutes – were required to undergo the usual early morning haircut carried out by the court barber and his curved razor.

Those left on the shortlist went on to part two – arrange those same 8 ladies as before with none in the same straight line, so that the numbers they stood on added up to the highest possible total.

Anyone who failed that test was taken to the nearest crossroads and despatched in four different directions!

Should any genius actually find the highest score then the trial was over and he won the princess's hand — what happened to the rest of her, history does not relate.

Since marriage to either princess (or both) is a better fate than any alternative, can you climb aboard your magic carpet, transport yourself to ancient Turkey, present yourself at the palace gates and win the hand of not one but both princesses?

FATIMA

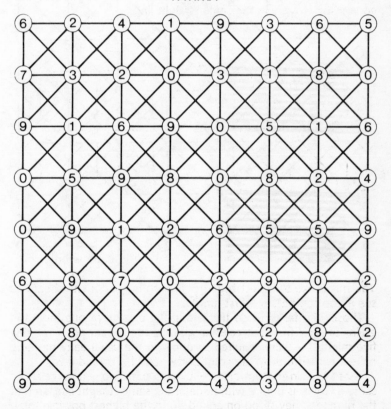

SOLUTION ON PAGE 190.

MINIMA

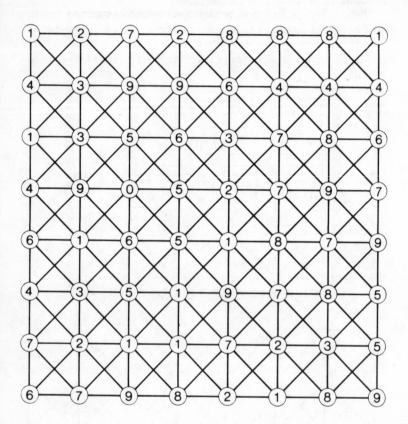

SOLUTION ON PAGE 190.

Square Around (???)

No, no need to look again. After a quick double take you have correctly realized there isn't a lot wrong with our friendly acknowledgement of your puzzling skills.

Just the L and A to switch around to make the bottom word PAL instead of PLA.

Unlike other good quality, sliding puzzles pouring out from the darkest depths of Taiwan, this one appears to be suffering from a major fault – with all nine squares occupied, how can anything slide?

Usually there is a spare square and we must admit that to have one would make things that much easier.

The best alternative on offer is to have two doors and a connecting corridor. The doors, though, are automatic.

Only one letter can pass through and occupy the corridor at any one time.

As the letter leaves the main area, the door it passes through locks so that the letter can only re-enter the grid by the other door. If you leave by one door you must enter by the other and vice versa.

Having shifted one letter into limbo, as it were, the other eight can be moved around until you, and they, are dizzy.

Then, when you wish it, make the square by the in-door empty and the letter can return.

A letter returning has the effect of unlocking the mechanism so either door can be used to move a letter out again.

As well as the problem given here you can make up your own using the same nine letter squares. Simply put them into the grid in any way you like and slide them around until they read

YOU
WIN
PAL

For any of these puzzles it is a sufficient achievement to complete the task but for those who like a stiffer challenge the main problem shown here can be solved in just 21 moves.

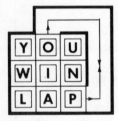  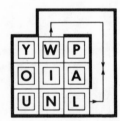

SOLUTION ON PAGE 189.

CALCULATOR'S CORNER

Don't panic! Only simple arithmetic is involved and no teacher will lean over you with a red pen to cross out your efforts. This chapter may even help children survive modern education.

Spot The Number (?)

This little game is a test of mental agility and can be played anywhere there is room to roll four dice by any number of players, young and old.

First of all, one player selects a target number, which should suit the age of the players and should probably not be more than about 300.

The four dice are rolled by another player and retrieved from under the carpet, the dog's left ear, Dad's beerglass or wherever else they have landed.

The four top numbers are noted and then used by the players, working against each other and a clock if you wish, to get as close to the target number as they can.

The rules are quite simple:

1) All four numbers must be used, once each.
2) The numbers may be added, subtracted, multiplied or divided.
3) The numbers may be combined together in pairs or even threes to form two and three-digit numbers.
4) A player who scores the target number gains three points. A player who forms a number which is within five of the target scores one point. (You may prefer to score highest points to the player nearest to the target, down to lowest points for the player furthest away — with, perhaps, a bonus for anyone actually making the target number exactly.)

Thus with a roll of ⚄ ⚀ ⚄ ⚄ it is possible to achieve a target number of 32 by using the 5 and the 3 to make 53, the 2 and the 1 make 21 and 53 − 21 = 32.

If the target was 96, then it can be scored by joining the 5 and 1 to make 51; 51 − 3 = 48 and 48 × 2 = 96.

A game can be as many rounds as there are players, so each has a turn rolling the dice, or an agreed number of rounds.

In our little competition your aim is to score 30 points in the 10 rounds. Can you do it?

	DIE ROLL				TARGET
A	⚀	⚁	⚃	⚅	**32**
B	⚂	⚁	⚄	⚂	**20**
C	⚀	⚃	⚃	⚅	**1**
D	⚁	⚄	⚂	⚅	**33**
E	⚂	⚃	⚁	⚄	**13**
F	⚁	⚂	⚂	⚂	**32**
G	⚄	⚄	⚄	⚅	**605**
H	⚁	⚃	⚄	⚄	**277**
I	⚀	⚂	⚅	⚁	**29**
J	⚅	⚅	⚅	⚅	**111**

SOLUTION ON PAGES 190 to 191.

Sum Score (?)

If we were to ask you to use three 3's to make 3, then there would be no problem, would there?

Instead we will ask you to make a variety of digital delights using the same digits.

To combine the digits you are allowed to use $+$, $-$, $\times$, and $\div$ and you may throw brackets around to make things clear.

The aim is not just to achieve the number but to use the simplest methods, so rate your efforts as follows:

If you use $\div$ anywhere score just 1 point for that answer.
If you use $\times$ anywhere, score 3 points.
If you use only $+$, $-$, then score top marks of 5 points.

So if you were to make 3 from three 3's by the sum $3 \times 3 \div 3$ you would gain just one point. But if you came up with $3 + 3 - 3$ that would be worth five points. You can, of course, put the digits together to make numbers, such as 555.

On your marks, then off for a quick sprint through these five posers.

    A. Use four 4's to make 44.
    B. Use five 5's to make 55.
    C. Use six 6's to make 66.
    D. Use seven 7's to make 77.
    E. Use eight 8's to make 88.

Cash, Bang, Wallet (?)

When incredibly rich business man, Augustus Monge, threw a firework party last November he spared no expense in ordering a personal stock of fireworks which would let the world know just what a price he was paying for this spectacular entertainment.

As each firework reached for the sky it exploded in a shower of stars which showed coin values large enough to be seen a mile or more away. Augustus' idea was that as each gem went off his friends could work out the price as they enjoyed its display.

Which made it all the more of a pity when his deputy-under-gardener, 'Erbert by name, acting as fire-raiser and reluctant at the enforced overtime, let off three fireworks at once.

SOLUTION ON PAGE 192.

As they shot upwards the cascading stars became so intermingled that it could not be seen just how much each had cost.

Still Augustus just had time before all went black to sack 'Erbert and tell his gathering that each firework had produced five stars; that the three were of three different prices, though the prices were equally spaced out and had cost a total of £1.50.

The cheapest had cost 43p; the Silver Drops had more 2p stars than did the Cascade and the Etna did not produce any 2p stars at all.

The company looked at each other and wrinkled their brows. It was beyond them, but it shouldn't be beyond you to work out which coins made up each starburst and the cost of each firework.

Magic Switch (?)

12	13	14	15
8	9	10	11
4	5	6	7
0	1	2	3

Magic squares, as we all know, have rows, columns and diagonals which add up to the same total. Which is a state our square completely fails to achieve.

Still, you can turn it into a genuine magic square by switching two of the numbers over.

Then doing that again. And again. Once more. Yes, making just four switches of pairs of numbers will do the trick!

When you have done it all the straight lines of four numbers will add up to 30.

	9		
		6	
0			

We have even placed three of the numbers for you. Can you place the rest?

SOLUTION ON PAGE 191.

Jolly Good Show (?)

At the Much Muddling Comprehensive School the maths teacher, Mr Jolly (known to his class as 'Freezer'), believes in making 'tables' practice as interesting as possible.

Instead of weekly tests he gives his class Tables Squares where most of the numbers are missing and just enough put in to enable the children to work out what goes where.

Since the weekly chore is followed by Games the children want to get the job done as quickly as possible. They have worked out that the quicker they can find the numbers which go around the edge, the faster they can fill in the middle.

How long do you need to complete each table?

EXAMPLE: ADDITION

$$4 + 3 = 7$$

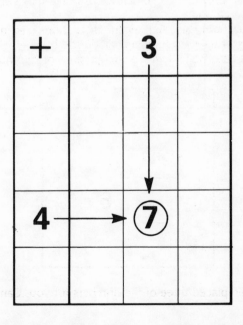

EXAMPLE: MULTIPLICATION

$$4 \times ? = 12$$

$$4 \times 3 = 12$$

×			③	
4			12	

ADDITION

Numbers to put round the edge: 0 to 9.

+	8	5			
			7	16	
4					
1					3
		11			
	11			12	

SOLUTION ON PAGE 192.

ADDITION

Numbers to put round the edge: 0 to 9.

+					
				13	
		1			**2**
			15		
		7		**15**	
			12		

SOLUTION ON PAGE 192.

MULTIPLICATION

Numbers to put round the edge: 0 to 9.

×					
	35	**42**			**21**
			18		
	5			**8**	
			8		

MULTIPLICATION

Numbers to place round the edge:
1 to 9 across the top.
1 to 9 down the side.

×									
				28					35
					2				
		12							
								30	
			16						
	8								
			6						
								36	
				81					

SOLUTION ON PAGE 192.

Sum Total (?)

Can you just pop the digits 1 to 9 into the square so that each line has the total given at the end of it?

To give you a start, three numbers are already in position.

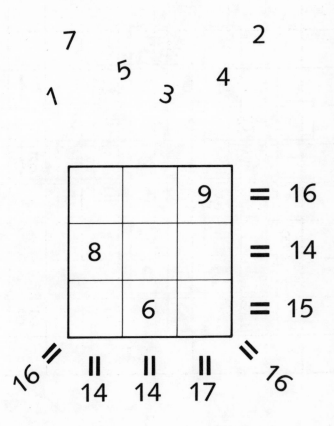

SOLUTION ON PAGE 192.

Sum Trouble (?)

In this rather weird grid, four sums going across the page have been mixed up with another four going down the page. From those which are already in position, can you work out where the rest of the figures and signs must be placed to make everything correct?

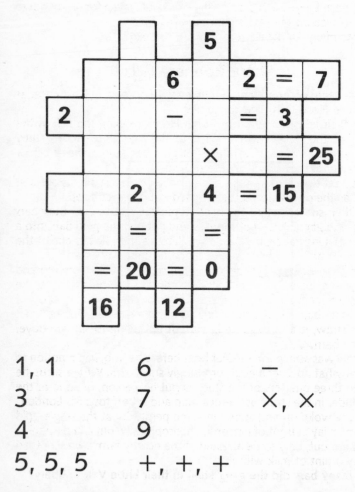

1, 1	6	−
3	7	×, ×
4	9	
5, 5, 5	+, +, +	

Fare, Please (??)

There never are more than 50 passengers on the one vehicle run by the Ben Nevis Bus Kompany but it was extraordinary when they all paid the same fare one day and offered exactly the same seven coins each, which made up the correct amount.

At the only stopping point, the driver noted that the total given by his machine was £9.79 and a quick riffle through the bag showed there wasn't a single 20p coin which he could swap for his own two 10ps for use on the café's chocolate machine.

So how many 2p coins were there in the bag?

Share Robbery (??)

You've heard of 'honour among thieves'? Forget it, at least as far as the Black Head Gang are concerned.

On their latest imitation of Robin Hood, robbing the rich in the shape of the bullion van to give to the poor, themselves, they actually got away with a number of gold bars and escaped across country until they found a deserted barn.

They set their loot in a pile and formed an uneasy ring around it, each, as their eyes closed, determined not to go to sleep.

As their snores forced the mice to put their paws over their ears one of the gang, Alf, crept forward and put half the gold bars into a bag. As an insurance, in case he was later caught, he hid one of the remaining bars in the straw and made his getaway.

Not long afterwards Clogger stirred, blinked, looked around and then made his way to the pile, which didn't seem as big as he vaguely remembered it, took two thirds of the gold bars and put them in his bag, He, too, took one bar from the remainder and hid it in the straw, just in case, and, without bothering to say goodbye, left the barn.

Ferdie was asleep for another hour before he, too, had a notion to look at what now seemed a surprisingly small haul. With a shrug he loaded three quarters of the stack about his person, hid one of the remainder in the straw as a precaution and set off towards London.

Jimmy woke up and stared in some perplexity at the single gold bar which lay in front of him and, philosophically, put it in his pocket and went out, only to be arrested at the nearby farm when he tried to buy a pint of milk with it.

How many bars did the gang steal in their Little Van Robbery?

SOLUTIONS ON PAGES 191 AND 192.

Digital Splits (??)

1 2 3 4 5 6 7

There are quite a few ways to arrange these digits into a three-digit number and a four-digit number; 123 and 4567 being the most obvious.

What we are looking for is that the three-digit number must be a multiple of 4 and the four-digit number a multiple of 3.

(Remember multiples? 12 is a multiple of 3 because 3 divides exactly into it.)

Your efforts in this direction will score points, equal to your two numbers added together.

For example, 5421 is a multiple of 3 and that leaves 736 as a multiple of 4 so the score is 5421 + 736 which is 6157.

How would you pop the digits into these boxes to make the score the highest possible?

A.

3-digit multiple of 4   4-digit multiple of 3

Now try these: again, how high a total can you manage? (By the way, double value in all these problems as you can go on to find the lowest total in each case — no extra charge either.)

B. 2 3 4 5 6 7 8

3-digit multiple of 4   4-digit multiple of 5

C. 7 6 5 4 3 2 1 0

4-digit multiple of 5

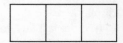

4-digit multiple of 6

D. 1 2 3 4 5 6 7 8 9

3-digit multiple of 3

3-digit multiple of 4

3-digit multiple of 5

E. 9 8 7 6 5 4 3 2

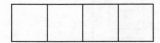

4-digit multiple of 8

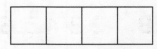

4-digit multiple of 9

SOLUTIONS ON PAGE 191.

Top Display (??)

Let the sad tale of Xavier Quidds serve as a lesson to us all.

In a lifetime spent watching what he spends and always going for the bargain, usually offered to him on a backstreet corner from the depths of a seedy-looking overcoat, he has amassed the biggest pile of junk seen outside a city tip this century.

Like this calculator, which does light up when switched on and will, if you are very careful, perform a sum or two.

Xavier has learned the hard way (he bought a gross of these!) that to avoid disaster when a key has been pressed, the next key hit must not be in the same row or column. If it is, the calculator shoots all its buttons at the user's face and expires with an electronic whine.

For instance, if you hit the 8 button you could not then hit 7, 9, or X, nor could you hit 5, 2 or +.

In any case, after hitting a number key you must then hit an operation key, then a number again, an operation key and so on.

If you are allowed to press only ten keys and a different one each time, what is the largest number you can make appear on the crystal display?

(PS: the last key you hit must be the = sign, or the number won't come up on the display at all!)

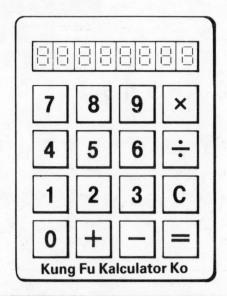

Kung Fu Kalculator Ko

SOLUTION ON PAGE 192.

SOLUTIONS

To make sure you don't 'accidentally' see the next answer, the solutions within each chapter have been muddled up.

ODD ONE OUT

2
FIFTY-FOUR. The others are all 'square' numbers' 1 × 1; 3 × 3; 5 × 5; 6 × 6; 9 × 9.

9
7011. In each of the other numbers the digits add up to eight.

1
D. This is a left hand and all the rest are of a right hand or foot.

8
SCREAM. Each of the others has three vowels and three con-sonants.

15
MICHAEL. The others are forenames of recent British Prime Ministers; James Callaghan; Edward Heath; Harold Macmillan; Anthony Eden and Sir Alec Douglas-Home.

4
ORANGE. If you have all the others and a large flat table you can enjoy a game of snooker.

20
CUBE C. C contradicts E so one of those is wrong and thus the others are all correct. E agrees with F so C is the odd one out.

3
D. GOOSE. The rest are birds of prey but you are not in any real danger of being eaten by a goose – rather the other way round!

10
1749. In all the others the number formed by the first two figures divides exactly into the number formed by the last two. Thus in 1976 – 19 goes into 76 four times.

16

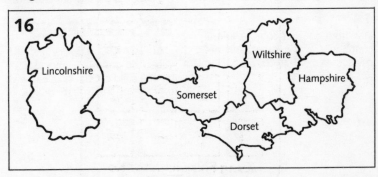

5

VENUS. Score ten bonus marks for all the reasons which make Venus such an odd planet. Here, the main reason is that all the other planets in this list have moons. But you may know that on all the planets except Venus the year is longer than the day. On Venus each day (one spin on its axis) is actually longer than one year (time taken to make one orbit of the Sun).

11

LIBRA. The sign of this astrological item is an object – a pair of scales. The other signs are of creatures. Pisces = fish. Cancer = crab. Taurus = bull. Capricorn = goat and Scorpio = scorpion.

17

B does not quite belong. The others are all rotations of each other but B is a reflection of the basic pattern.

13

D is an Alsatian. The other dogs all begin with B: Boxer, Bloodhound, Bull Terrier, Basset Hound.

18

D is from another cube. A and D contradict so the other four are correct. D contradicts B so D is wrong.

12

E is somewhat different. For all the others the squares are always on *opposite* sides of the same arm and the circles are on the same side. On E this is reversed.

7

MONSOON is a season and a rainy one to boot; the others will give you the wind up.

19

R. The rest are the position letters of girls in a netball team; WA = Wing Attack and so on. (No, boys, don't complain – you really ought to know. After all you probably bore your girlfriend silly with talk of sweepers, midfield and front runners!)

6

WEST. All the rest are seas: Black Sea; North Sea; Red Sea; Dead Sea.

14

SALE. The others are official abbreviations of American states; ALASka, MASSachusetts and so on.

BITS & PIECES

HALF-CAKED IDEA

What the good lady should do is let one child cut the cake and give the other child first choice of pieces!

STRAWBERRY SHARES

11

1

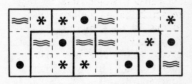

7

10

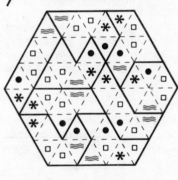

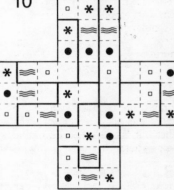

4

3

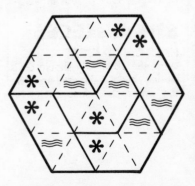

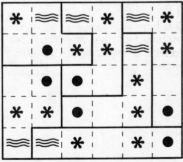

9

6

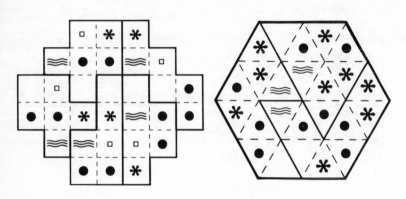

12

2

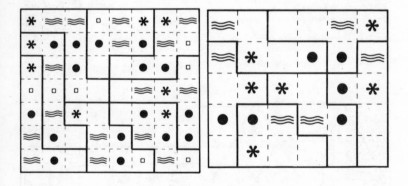

5

8

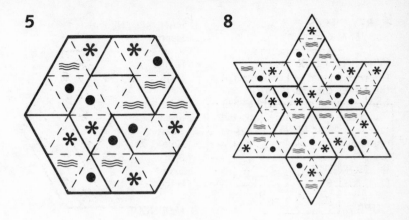

SPOT THE DIFFERENCE

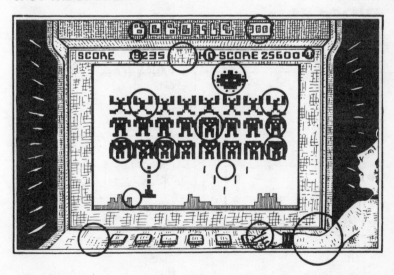

PARTY PIECES
B, D, E, A, C.

WINNING CUT
Cheryl, with that one swift flash of the knife, cut the board in half from left to right, turned her half round which meant her King could take all of her father's pieces in one move.

IN SEQUENCE
D, E, A, C, B.

CUBE BITS
Yes, it can be made.

RIDDLES
WHAT'S MY BLANK?

3 **SUGAR**
Season
Ugly
Gas
Apple
Rag

2 **POTATO**
Panel
Option
Toffee
Arch
Toe
Orange

1 **LION**
Left
Island
Offer (Occasion)
Navy

6 **HANDKERCHIEF**
Heart
Anvil
Nights
Dish
Killer
Extra
Road
Coast
Hole
Inch
Easter
Fingers

8 **MERINGUE**
Moon
Engine
Ring
Invaders
Note
Goal
Under
Ear

4 **CANDY FLOSS**
ClifF
ApriL
NO
DresS
YearS

7 **PINE TREE**
PinT
InneR
NettlE
EyE

5 **CHIP SHOP**
ClasS
HigH
IntO
PumP

FILM FUN
The Umpire Strikes Back.
Return Of The Jetty.
20,000 Leeks Under The Sea.
Merry Poppings.
From Russia With Glove and Coldfinger.

WHAT'S YOURS?
Bed. (Flower bed, bed you sleep in, and river or sea bed.)

GET THIS
A golf course.

THE PLACE TO BE
Address.

BLEEP, BLEEP
A space set alight (space satellite!).

ONE, TWO, THREE...
Ewe.

SPOT THIS ONE
A die. It has the numbers 1 to 6 in spots, the total is 21.

WHAT IS IT?
The Earth.

A WORD FROM THE BARD
Water.

ACROSS THE GREAT DIVIDE
Just after she had suffered a fatal heart attack, Edwina's body was transported on a plane and crossed the International Date Line! Upon which Monday changed back to Sunday.

GARDENERS' QUESTION TIME
Carrot. Car, arr, rot.

A FIR QUESTION
Superman, otherwise Clark Kent.

CODEWORD

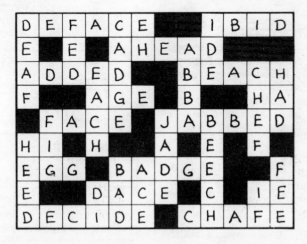

CALLING ALL PUZZLERS
Let your brain take the strain.

JUNGLE JESTER
Monkey.

HEADLESS RHYME
There was a young man from Dee
Who went for a swim in the sea.
A shark saw his flippers
And said 'whoopee kippers!'
Then ate the young man for his
  tea.

CRASHWORD
Washing machine.

CODESQUARE

START

TENOR

ANGLE

ROLES

TRESS

THE STORY SO FAR
Tracey Scott and her friends, Christopher and Sandra Edwards, carefully turned the key to the warehouse door. Slowly it began to open, groaning and growling like a bear disturbed during its winter sleep.

Inside the darkness crowded around our scared heroes; scampering noises set their teeth chattering in fright. Somewhere in this vast building the crooks had stashed the gold bullion.

As they groped their way along a musty, smelly wall, a switch clicked on and a brilliant shaft of light played on them.

They were trapped!

WHO DID WHAT?
THE SEASIDE SAGA

Sarah	funfair	mother
Brian	ice cream	grandad
Tim	pier	aunt
Joan	donkey ride	uncle

ROAD UP

house	name
A	Sangster
B	Dennett
C	Thomas
D	Hughes
E	Ready
F	Adams
G	Briscoe
H	Flower

MINOR LEAGUE

Bill	Bears	1
Fred	Giants	2
Leslie	Allstars	3
Tony	Bluesox	4

FLASH CRASH

The winner was Phil Davies in the Zoom. The rest of the details are:

Clive	Morelli	Streak	No fuel
John	Chappell	Lightning	Fire
Max	Bennett	Flash	Oil patch
Steve	Quest	Jet	Lost bend

FRUIT & VEG

The carrots should be in the middle row in the third box from the left. The entire display should be laid out as follows:

plums	lettuce	apples	sprouts
cabbage	oranges	carrots	pears
peaches	cucumber	grapes	potatoes

DAYLIGHT ROBBERY

Mr Lomond	Van	High Street	Knoyle View
Miss Hammett	Sports	West Way	High Street
Mrs Green	Estate	Long Lane	West Way
Mr Wilkins	Saloon	Bradley Road	Long Lane
Miss Lever	Mini	Knoyle View	Bradley Road

Miss Hammett in the sports car and Mr Lomond in the van may, to use a marvellous understatement, be able to assist the police with their enquiries.

RING O ROSE'S

Reading clockwise around the ring, the children are; Rose, Andrew, Tanya, Edward, Sarah, Colin.

TAKE IT FROM HERE

Alice	Hooper	chow mein	34
Bill	Jackson	chop suey	45
Charles	Goldsmith	special	16
Dora	Innis	foo young	21
Eileen	Farley	prawn rice	52

AMAZING MAZES

CLUED BRICK CUBE

DEVINE INTERVENTION

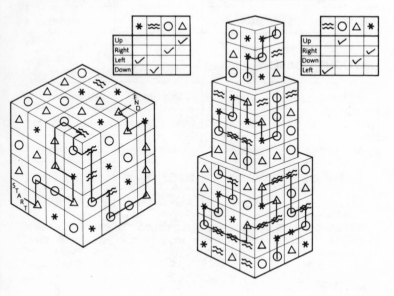

RED RIDING ROUTE

The shortest path is shown here. If you left the shops by going left, up, right, then your path is a bit longer and the wolf will be at Grannie's door!

HOME 1	1	5	4	3	3	1	6
0	1	0	1	2	2	3	4
3	5	4	1	SHOPS 1	2	0	4
0	1	1	0	4	2	1	1
2	WOODS 1	5	2	0	3	3	3
0	0	2	1	3	4	3	6
2	3	2	2	4	1	0	GRANNIE'S

THE MARSH OF MYNOG

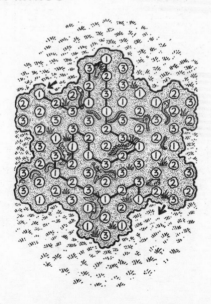

DRUNKEN ANT

Including the end, the alcoholic ant travelled through 45 squares on his journey. (And this must be his actual path.)

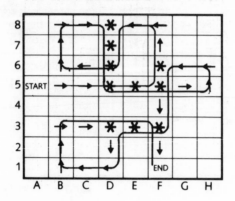

58 squares. (Again the genuine route.)

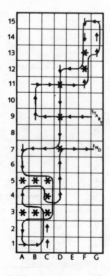

75 moves in this one but your beginning may not be the same as this sample.

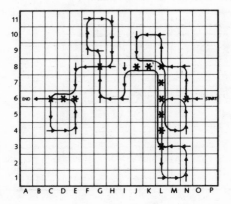

This shows one of several possible routes which take 124 squares.

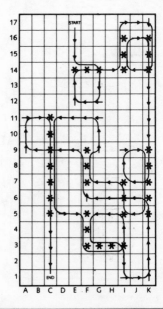

MAZE PHRASE OF PHILOS

In this chart F means forward towards the centre of the spiral and B backwards towards Start.

F3	F5	B3	B3	F5	B3	F5	F3	F3	F3	B5
R	E	D	*	S	K	Y	*	A	T	*

F3	B5	F3	F3	F3	F3	F5	B3	B3	B3	F5
N	I	G	H	T	*	Y	O	U	R	*

F3	F3	F5	F3	B5	F3	B5	B5	F3	F3	F5	B3	F5	F3	
R	O	O	F	*	I	S	*	A	L	I	G	H	T	END

SUM MAZE

Here is a way to score 49 points. Any advance?

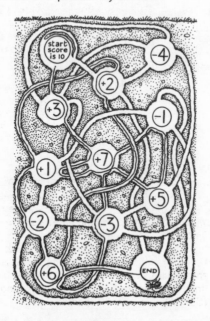

INITIATIVE TESTS

TIME FOR THE BUS
The 6.18 is bus number 3. The number of each bus is the hour it departs divided into the minutes: thus 3 into 24 goes 8.

FRUIT SALAD
Grape; apple; lemon; peach. The letters of each word are set out in alternate squares.

SWITCH WORD
Heights is in the wrong group and should join the other. Outworn, listening, money and canine all have numbers spelled out within them, as does h*eight*s.

DON'T TOUCH
S. Going round the square in a spiral from the top right hand corner spells DANGEROUS.

GET THE PICTURE
D. The King of Spades. In each line across and down the faces look alternatively left and right. Of the four remaining court cards only the King of Spades looks right.

LINKS
C: Flower. In each line across the middle picture has a link with the two either side:
WALL PAPER WEIGHT
(wallpaper and paperweight)
NOSE BAG PIPE
(nosebag and bagpipe)
Flower completes sunflower and flowerbed.

PICK A PIC
B: the belt. the pictures show
Match, ?, Pin
Bolt   Cup
Each word has just one vowel; A, I, O, U. Only Belt had E to complete the set of vowels.

CUP TIED
Bert did not win the treble chance as the result was DERBY 1 PLYMOUTH 2. The score by each team is simply the number of vowels in that team's printed name.

MEET THE DEALER
Seattle Square: five of clubs. Each row contains one of each suit and the numbers increase by two each time.
Denver Diamond: two of spades. Each line of 3 cards totals 15. Cards above the value of a five are all diamonds and the rest are spades.

Toledo Triangle: King of clubs. The number value of each card is found by adding together the values of the two cards above it. The suits hearts, clubs, diamonds, spades, spiral from left to right.

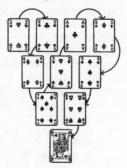

NUMBER PLEASE
The missing number is 3. Either you can see the series 1; 1, 2; 1, 2, 3; 1, 2, 3, 4; 1, 2, 3, 4, 5 going clockwise around the rectangle or you could say that there are five 1's, four 2's, two 4's and one 5. So a 3 is needed to make three 3's.

JEKYLL & HYDE
Reading diagonally left to right the letters spell MORECAMBE AND WISE.

MISSING LINK
C: the bun. In each line across the three words rhyme:

Tune	Gun	Car
Moon	Sun	Star
Balloon.	Bun.	Jar.

MISSING FOUR
The letters have been sown in every other square starting from the top left corner and returning to the adjacent square when the bottom right corner is reached.

A	I	B	J
K	C	L	D
E	M	F	N
O	G	P	H

NINEWORDS
1. Marmalade.
2. Telescope.
3. Badminton.
4. Delicious.
5. Exploring.
6. Noiseless.
7. Overspend.
8. Yesterday.
9. Acrobatic.

POETIC JUSTICE
Lady Silvia da Quincy did the foul deed. The first and last letters of each line form her name.

IN THE PICTURE
B: the book. The middle picture in each line acts as a link between the two end pictures.
Handcuff – cufflink.
Applecart – cartwheel.
Logbook – bookworm.

WHODUNNIT?

SPEAR MURDER
Bert Crabtree, the plumber, was in the library and did the dirty deed. For the record, the others were disposed as follows:
Conservatory — Hon Histodd. Dining room — Miss Spinks. TV Room — Tara Lotte. Morning Room — Lavinia Scrownge. Music Room — Sir Arthur Legoffe. Billiards Room — Gravell. Cloakroom — Elspeth. Lounge — Lady Tayble.

PIC FIT THREE	E
PIC FIT TWO	D
PIC FIT ONE	B
PIC FIT FOUR	C

VICTORY ON PAPER
Harry Scott is holding the cup. In all the pictures he is the only left-hander.

THE LONG SHOT
No, Alphonse did not get away with it and was convicted of murder.

The witness only heard one shot yet two were fired. If the shots sounded simultaneous to him then the man who was a long way away must have fired first for the sound of his shot to reach the witness's ears at the same time as the sound from the nearby gun.

VISITING TIME
Marie Suggett, the director's wife, is the guilty party.

The four couples are: Sonia and Cedric Davies, surgeon. Clare and James Finch, broker. Alison and Andrew Marsh, painter. Marie and Peter Suggett, director.

The schedule was:
8.40 Mr Davies, Mr Finch and Mrs Davies went in.
8.50 Mrs Davies left. Mr Suggett, Mr Marsh, Mrs Finch went in.
9.05 Messrs Davies, Marsh, Suggett left, then Mrs Suggett went in.
9.30 Mr and Mrs Finch left — leaving Mrs Suggett alone in the room with the patient before Mrs Marsh went in.
9.50 Mrs Marsh and Mrs Suggett left.

OPEN AND SHUT CASE
The man with the hat should be arrested. His case is identical to the one in the picture, the others differ in some detail of the zips around the case and pocket.

CROMWELL'S REVENGE
The sentry on duty had committed the terrible crime of being asleep cat his post! How else could he have 'just had a dream'?

TRUTH WILL OUT
If you have popped in for a bit of help, let us just rid ourselves of the rest by saying straight away: Alf drove the van, Bert bunged the brick and Charlie waved the gun around. Alf told the truth, Bert told one lie and Charlie told two lies.

Right. Have the clever clogs gone? Good, gather round.

The secret is simply to assume that one of the three told the truth — so pick anybody you like and treat their remarks as if they are correct. Who would you like? Bert? He'll do.

If Bert told the truth then Alf drove the van, Charlie threw the brick and so Bert must have waved the gun around.

Check these 'facts' against Alf's statements.

He says he drove the van — which would be true — and Bert threw the brick — which would be false. OK so far.

Now check Charlie's statements.

Bert waved the gun around — which would be true — and Charlie drove the van — which would be false.

So if Bert is telling the truth then the other two have told one lie each, which we are informed did not happen.

So Bert is not the truth teller.

If you take Charlie's statements to be true you will find that both Alf and Bert told two lies — so Charlie is not the truth teller either.

Therefore Alf must have told the truth — which means Alf drove, Bert bunged and Charlie waved.

All clear? Jolly good. Off you go then.

LORRY LOAD OF LIES
Barry was the guest of honour at the local magistrates court.

DOUBLE TROUBLE
Slugger tried to break the lock. Toddy sprayed the gas. Ugly rammed the van.

CAUGHT NAPPING
Mugsy set the ladder up. Patsy wrote the note. Sudsy climbed in the window.

SWEET REASON
Marcus took the sweets and Marcus also ran away with them. No matter which of the two boys lies completely both lead to Marcus taking the bag. So that makes Sheila's first statement true. Therefore she lied when she said that Johnny ran off with it. So Marcus must have done, naughty lad.

SHOPPING AROUND
Jenny created the diversion while Karen passed the goods to Helen who took them out of the shop.

DON'T BANK ON IT
Joe guarded the staff. Klive grabbed the cash. Limey cut the alarm.

FRAUDULENT CONVERSION
Fergus collected the money from the bank. Gerald changed the computer program. Howard copied the key.

PEACH SURPRISE
Sid Woodward was murdered by Charles Dent.

Reading clockwise around the table, the dinner party was:
Eric Carter: steak and ice cream.

Phil England: pork chop and cheese.
Bert Hunter: game pie and fresh fruit.
Sid Woodward: duck and quite a peach surprise.
Charles Dent: trout and trifle.

TEAM GAMES

FUR ENOUGH

The lady had weighed herself and been dissatisfied with the machine's verdict. She was about to try again when she suddenly had what she thought was a brainwave. She took off her heavy fur coat and carefully placed it over her arm before stepping back on the scales! She was very disappointed to see it made no difference to her weight.

RIDDLE OF THE CRYING MAN

One man is a prisoner, the other a prison officer. The convict had taken the advantage of a roadside stop to pull a gun on the guard and demand that the handcuffs binding them together be opened. The officer decided to make a fight of it and put the key in his mouth to free his one usable hand and tackle the gunman. In panic the prisoner shot him and the officer *swallowed the key*. So the criminal cannot get away from the man he has just killed.

UNLUCKY THIRTEEN

Take a deep breath for this one . . . The man was simply a very, very *bad conductor*!

FIELD FIND

Vincent made his journey in early spring soon after the snow had melted. The same snow which the village children had used to make a snowman which they decorated with coal for eyes, nose and coat buttons and carrot for a mouth.

DASH IT

The lady in the house was an actress rehearsing an Agatha Christie thriller. She was practising her dying screams for the end of act one and the passing man had thought it real and rushed in to save her.

FIRST – AND LAST – ORDER

The man had hiccups. He asked for a glass of water to cure them but the barman knew that a sudden shock is also a good cure. So he pulled the gun. The method worked and the man thanked him for his medicinal help.

LATE LAMENTED

Fred and Freda are, or rather were, goldfish. It was the cat who had pulled the cloth on which their bowl was standing, sending it crashing to the floor and causing the startled feline to make a quick exit.

THE HOUSE CALL

Henry Kingsbury, shame on him, was a burglar. He had entered the unlit house by a back window and made his way to the lounge. The glowing fire reminded him how cold he was so he thought he would warm up before doing his dastardly deeds.

He was shocked when a voice behind him said 'Stick 'em up!' and, being non-violent, he did. What caused his collapse was when the voice continued by saying 'Have a nut,' and 'Who's a pretty boy, then?' and he realized he had been arrested by the owner's parrot.

DOMESTIC TIFF
Mrs Platt did outwork for a computer firm and had to thread 3,000 components onto the wire. After a tiring evening threading and counting she was near the end of her labours when the telehone rang. Her husband answered it and said 'Hello. Sicklehampton 2496.' She lost count.

KNEES DOWN
Two five-a-side football teams plus one referee are searching for a contact lens lost by one of the players.

AH – AGH!
As I heard it, this was a true story which happened a long time ago. The two men were playing chess and one suddenly saw a move which would give him checkmate. He stood up in triumph but forgot that, absorbed in the game, he had wrapped a leg around the leg of the table. Standing up like that severely damaged his leg. (No mention is made of what happened to the table.)

All of which proves that even chess can be a dangerous game.

THE DEATH CALL
The man was a fisherman and had just made the catch of a lifetime. He had phoned his wife to tell her about it and she had, naturally, asked how big the fish was. He answered, like every angler before him, with his arms. His last words as his hands went through the glass which slashed his wrists were: 'It was THAT big!'

DOWN – AND OUT
The man has found a very rare parking space so he has sent his wife to fetch the family car.

STRINGING YOU ALONG
The couple were on a long ride late at night and their windscreen wiper motor had broken. The lady had tied a string to each wiper blade and for many miles she had tugged back and forth to keep the blades going.

I could not supply or fit another motor so they just had to keep going.

SHORT STOP
We were looking for the way to open the bonnet. The man had borrowed the car from a friend who told him it needed oil. He didn't like to call in and just ask for help since he could not find the bonnet catch himself so he bought the petrol first and then asked.

I don't recall what make of car it was, it had a wooden fascia, but though we searched all over neither of us could find a way to get the bonnet open.

A FERRY CLOSE AFFAIR

The officer told our young leaper that the ferry was coming in, not leaving as he had supposed.

A MOVING EXPERIENCE

He is standing on an underground escalator trying to pencil in a beard and moustache on an advertisement's face. As the escalator descends he must lean forward and eventually run back up a few steps in order to stay where he is. When he has finished he stands still and the machinery takes him down.

BUS STOP

The bus was on a through route from Wolverhampton to Worcester. The man had joined the bus at Wolverhampton and asked for a ticket to Birmingham. Unfortunately he fell asleep before reaching that city.

He was still asleep when the conductor came to ask for the fares. On being woken up he did not believe that he had slept right through Birmingham and insisted that he had already paid his fare.

Eventually he saw the light and the conductor kindly stopped the bus opposite a stop where the man could catch a bus back to Birmingham.

LITTLE BOY BLUE

The lad told the policeman that he had run away from home but was not yet old enough to cross the road.

CARDBOARD & COUNTERS

COIN OP

(Or its mirror image, switched left to right.)

20P	5P	1P
2P	50P	10P

CHANGE IN THE WEATHER

One way to do it in 22 moves:
2 to 7. 1 to 6. 7 to 1. 9 to 2. 8 to 4. 6 to 8. 4 to 6. 2 to 9. 1 to 7. 6 to 1. 3 to 6. 7 to 3. 9 to 2. 10 to 4. 6 to 10. 4 to 6. 2 to 9. 3 to 7. 6 to 3. 7 to 6. 9 to 2. 6 to 9.

SQUARE AROUND

The main problem can be solved in 21 moves if, at a particular stage, you move L in at one door and on the next move take L out again by the same door! Start by moving A out of the bottom door. Then move the following letters into the adjacent space: L, I, N, U, O and A in at the top door. L out at the bottom door. I, N, A moved into space left and L in at top door. L out at top door. O, U, I, N, A, I, N moved and L in at bottom door.

OVER KNIGHT STOP

Just 8 moves are needed:
A to E to F. I to E to A. C to D to I. H to G to D to C. B to G to H. F to E. J to F to B. E to F to J.

QUEENS HIGH

Fatima is yours if you scored 63 points by placing the queens at the circled numbers. Her sister requires a score of 67.

FATIMA

6 2 4 1 ⑨ 3 6 5
7 3 2 0 3 1 ⑧ 0
⑨ 1 6 9 0 5 1 6
0 5 ⑨ 8 0 8 2 4
0 9 1 2 6 5 5 ⑨
6 9 7 0 2 ⑨ 0 2
1 8 0 ① 7 2 8 2
9 ⑨ 1 2 4 3 8 4

MINIMA

1 2 7 2 8 ⑧ 8 1
4 3 ⑨ 9 6 4 4 4
1 3 5 6 3 7 ⑧ 6
4 ⑨ 0 5 2 7 9 7
6 1 6 5 1 8 7 ⑨
4 3 5 1 ⑨ 7 8 5
⑦ 2 1 1 7 2 3 5
6 7 9 ⑧ 2 1 8 9

HIGH DIE HI!

Fifty points can be scored in the 3 by 3 square as follows:
right, down, right, down, left, up, left, down, right, right, up, up, left, down, left, up.

6	**6**	**6**
6	**4**	**5**
6	**6**	**5**

Sixty points can be scored in the second problem by moving:

down, right, up, left, right, down, right, down, down, right, up, left, left, down, right, up, right, down, left, up, left, up, right, down, down, right, up, left, left, left, up.

5	**5**		
6	**6**	**6**	
6	**4**	**1**	**5**
	5	**5**	**6**

Can It Be Beaten?

To give you something to shoot at, here is a target of 69 points for the third picture:

down, right, up, left, right, down, right, down, right, up, left, down, left, left, up, down, right, up, down, right, right, right, up, left, down, left, up, right, right, up.

5	**5**			**6**
6	**6**	**6**	**2**	**6**
6	**6**	**5**	**4**	**6**

CALCULATOR'S CORNER

SPOT THE NUMBER

Thirty points are yours if you have these or an equally good alternative.

A. $3 \times 6 + 14$.
B. $23 - (5 - 2)$
C. $(4 - 1) - (6 - 4)$
D. $56 - 23$
E. $25 - (3 \times 4)$
F. $32 + (3 - 3)$
G. $(5 + 6) \times 55$
H. $554 \div 2$
I. $(3 + 2) \times 6 - 1$
J. $666 \div 6$

12	2	1	15
7	9	10	4
11	5	6	8
0	14	13	3

DIGITAL SPLITS

There is more than one way to de-fur this particular domestic pet so we give the top score (we hope!) and one way of achieving it.

A. 8173. $532 + 7641$.
B. 9377. $632 + 8745$.
C. 13942. $7510 + 6432$.
D. 2538 $861 + 932 + 745$.
E. 18197. $8432 + 9765$.

CASH, BANG, WALLET

Cascade: 1p, 2p, 10p, 10p, 20p.
            Cost: 43p
Etna: 5p, 5p, 10p, 10p, 20p.
            Cost: 50p
Rocket: 1p, 2p, 2p, 2p, 50p.
            Cost: 57p

MAGIC SWITCH

Switching four pairs of numbers which are symmetrically opposite through the centre will do the trick.

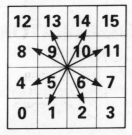

SUM TROUBLE

	6		5			
3	+	6	−	2	=	7
2	×	4	−	5	=	3
	5	×	1	×	5	=	25
9	+	2	+	4	=	15
	1	=	7	=		
	=	20	=	0		
	16		12			

SHARE ROBBERY

There were 56 bars in the original haul.

Jimmy found one, which added to the one hidden under the floor by Ferdie gives two, which is a quarter of the pile that crook found. So Ferdie found eight bars; add the one hidden by Clogger gives nine, which is one third of the heap which Clogger put his hands on. This gives 27 bars and again adding the 1 under the floorboard deposited by Alf gives 28, which is half the original pile.

SUM SCORE
A. 44 − (4 − 4) scores 5 points.
B. (5 × 5) + (5 × 5) + 5 scores 3 points.
C. 66 − 66 + 66 scores 5 points.
D. (7 × 7) + (7 × 7) − 7 − 7 − 7 scores 3 points.
E. 888 − 888 + 88 scores 5 points.

TOP DISPLAY
$9 \div 1 + 7 - 2 \times 6 = 84$

FARE PLEASE
Twenty-two 2p coins were in the bag.

The total fare in pence, 979, is 89 × 11. Since there never are many passengers it cannot mean 89 people paying 11p each so it must be 11 passengers paying 89p. However that amount is made up using seven coins, it must contain just two 2p coins.

SUM TOTAL

4	3	**9**	= 16
8	5	1	= 14
2	**6**	7	= 15

16 ‖ 14   ‖ 14   ‖ 17   16

JOLLY GOOD SHOW

MULTIPLICATION (2)

×	8	3	2	4	9	1	7	6	5
7	56	21	14	28	63	7	49	42	35
2	16	6	4	8	18	2	14	12	10
4	32	12	8	16	36	4	28	24	20
5	40	15	10	20	45	5	35	30	25
8	64	24	16	32	72	8	56	48	40
1	8	3	2	4	9	1	7	6	5
3	24	9	6	12	27	3	21	18	15
6	48	18	12	24	54	6	42	36	30
9	72	27	18	36	81	9	63	54	45

ADDITION (1)

+	8	5	0	9	2
7	15	12	7	16	9
4	12	9	4	13	6
1	9	6	1	10	3
6	14	11	6	15	8
3	11	8	3	12	5

MULTIPLICATION (1)

×	5	6	2	8	3
7	35	42	14	56	21
0	0	0	0	0	0
9	45	54	18	72	27
1	5	6	2	8	3
4	20	24	8	32	12

ADDITION (2)

+	3	1	7	9	2
4	7	5	11	13	6
0	3	1	7	9	2
8	11	9	15	17	10
6	9	7	13	15	8
5	8	6	12	14	7

GYLES BRANDRETH'S
PUZZLES
AND
BRAINTEASERS

INTRODUCTION

At school I had a teacher whose name – I promise you – was Justin Thyme. Though he taught geography for a living, he really lived not for his work but for his hobby which was collecting, devising and solving puzzles. I had him very much in mind while compiling this book because it contains all the kinds of puzzles he enjoyed most: word puzzles, number puzzles, picture puzzles, puzzles involving coins and dominoes and matchsticks. Mr Thyme liked plenty of variety in his puzzles and I know it would have delighted him to come across a book that included puzzles as amazing as most of our mazes (page 274), as baffling as some of our Brainteasers (page 280) and as unusual as all our Tangrams (page 330).

Every puzzle in the book has been given a star rating. The one-star puzzles are the easiest. The two-star puzzles are rather more taxing. And even Mr Thyme might find the three-star puzzles something of a challenge. I hope you enjoy them all. And to put you in the right mood let me start you off with one of Mr Thyme's favourites. He would come into the classroom, call for silence and then announce his Proverb of the Day:

A slight inclination of the cranium is as adequate as a spasmodic movement of one optic to an equine quadruped utterly devoid of any visionary capacity.

What on earth was he trying to say?

P.S. You will find the answer to Mr Thyme's puzzle with all the others at the back of the book.

WORD
UZZLES

WORD PLAY

Simple Start*

The longest word in the Oxford English Dictionary is this one:

PNEUMONOULTRAMICROSCOPICSILICOVOLCANOCONIOSIS

It is a 45 letter word that is the alleged name of a disease supposedly contracted from breathing in fine volcanic dust.

Here are some more words that are neither so long nor so difficult, but can you work out what each one means?

Verbal Display*

1. What is **to hustle?**
   Is it: a) to push and hurry?
   b) to go to sleep?
   c) to jump high in the air?
   d) to round up cattle?

2. What is **to brawl?**
   Is it: a) to sail a yacht?
   b) to sing loudly?
   c) to fight?
   d) to cook?

3. What is **to gratify?**
   Is it: a) to grate cheese?
   b) to laugh?
   c) to catch a cold?
   d) to please?

4. What is **to munch?**
   Is it: a) to be sick?
   b) to eat?
   c) to spit?
   d) to drink?

5. What is **to repulse?**
   Is it: a) to drive off an attack?
   b) to take a pulse for a second time?

SOLUTIONS ON PAGE 346.

c) to steal money?
d) to faint at the sight of blood?

6. What is **to submerge?**
   Is it: a) to climb mountains?
   b) to lift great weights?
   c) to go under water?
   d) to open a bank account?

7. What is **to distort?**
   Is it: a) to make something straight?
   b) to make something die?
   c) to put something out of shape?
   d) to bounce something up and down?

8. What is **to meditate?**
   Is it: a) To visit the Mediterranean?
   b) to administer medicine?
   c) to paint a picture?
   d) to think deeply?

9. What is **to wallop?**
   Is it: a) to serve ice-cream?
   b) to hit someone or something?
   c) to bite someone or something?
   d) to travel by kangaroo?

10. What is **to somnambulate?**
    Is it: a) to call an ambulance?
    b) to try to fly?
    c) to bury someone alive?
    d) to walk in one's sleep?

Collecting Collectives***

You probably know that a group of ants is called a colony and a collection of ponies is called a string, but did you know that a mass of larks is known as an **exaltation**? There are collective nouns to describe all sorts of groups of animals. On the next page is a list of some of the most interesting and unusual of these. The collective noun is provided, all you have to do is supply the names of the animals.

SOLUTIONS ON PAGE 346.

To help you the first letter of each of the animal names is given:

1. A shrewdness of a _ _ _   2. A cete of b _ _ _ _ _ _
3. A shoal of b _ _ _   4. A sloth of b _ _ _ _
5. An army of c _ _ _ _ _ _ _ _ _ _ _   6. A clowder of c _ _ _
7. A drove of c _ _ _ _ _   8. A peep of c _ _ _ _ _ _ _
9. A murder of c _ _ _ _   10. A dule of d _ _ _ _
11. A school of f _ _ _   12. A skulk of f _ _ _ _
13. A gaggle of g _ _ _ _   14. A husk of h _ _ _ _
15. A cast of h _ _ _ _   16. A brood of h _ _ _
17. A siege of h _ _ _ _ _   18. A haras of h _ _ _ _ _ _
19. A smack of j _ _ _ _ _ _ _ _   20. A kindle of k _ _ _ _ _ _
21. A deceit of l _ _ _ _ _ _ _   22. A leap of l _ _ _ _ _ _ _
23. A pride of l _ _ _ _   24. A plague of l _ _ _ _ _ _
25. A watch of n _ _ _ _ _ _ _ _ _ _   26. A parliament of o _ _ _

Homophones*

No, homophones aren't telephones you have around the house: they are words that sound alike, but have different spellings or different meanings – like **wholly** (meaning 'completely') and **holy** (meaning 'sacred'). Can you find the homophones that will fit these clues?

1. a. **The opposite of left**   b. **A special kind of ceremony**
   Both words begin with letter R.

2. a. **A group of musicians**   b. **Forbidden**
   Both words begin with B.

3. a. **Corn on the cob**   b. **A Labyrinth you might get lost in.**
   Both words begin with M.

4. a. **To agree**   b. **A climb**
   Both words begin with A.

5. a. **When you break the rules in a sport**
   b. **This is what a chicken is**
   Both words begin with F.

SOLUTIONS ON PAGES 346 AND 347.

6. a. An agreement   b. What a suitcase is when it's full
   Both words begin with P.

7. a. A cricketer does it.
   b. You eat soup out of it.
   Both words begin with B.

8. a. You can bounce it   b. Shout
   Both words begin with B.

9. a. A river in France   b. Rational health
   Both words begin with S.

10. a. To put in position   b. A flattened fish.
    Both words begin with P.

WHAT LETTER WOULD BE USEFUL
TO A DEAF WOMAN?

THE LETTER A BECAUSE IT MAKES
HER HEAR

SOLUTIONS ON PAGE 347.

ANAGRAMS

If you were given the following phrases:

A smart giant, Ma!

Matt sang 'Maria'.

Mama's a ratting.

Gain a smart mat.

apart from the fact that they make little sense, you would probably feel that they have little in common. Wrong! If the letters in each phrase are transposed the word ANAGRAMMATIST can be formulated, which is exactly what you would be if you did so! See how great your skill as an anagrammatist is with the following variety of puzzles.

Head Over Heels*

Take the words **ROAST MULES** and rearrange the ten letters in the words to form a single ten-letter word.

European Cities**

Here are anagrams of 14 European cities. How quickly can you discover their names? (As a clue the country in which you will find the city is given in brackets.)

1. EVINCE (Italy)
2. PANELS (Italy)
3. HASTEN (Greece)
4. MISER (France)
5. ANISE (Italy)
6. SABLE (Switzerland)
7. PAIRS (France)
8. ROCK (Eire)
9. SOLO (Norway)
10. MORE (Italy)
11. ENGLARDIN (USSR)
12. LOOTED (Spain)
13. STONED (Belgium)
14. AVENGE (Switzerland)

World Cities***

Today Europe, tomorrow the world! Unscramble the names of the following cities around the globe. (Again the countries in which you will find the cities are given in brackets.)

SOLUTIONS ON PAGES 347 AND 348.

1. MINKS (USSR)
2. SAULT (USA)
3. UNITS (Tunisia)
4. GOALS (Nigeria)
5. BAULK (Afghanistan)
6. LOUSE (Vietnam)
7. MAILS (India)
8. MAIL (Peru)
9. NERO (USA)
10. SALVAGES (USA)
11. DIAGNOSE (USA)
12. DOTTIER (USA)
13. JUANITA (Mexico)
14. GRANITE (Morocco)
15. COUNTS (USA)
16. ANTHER (Iran)
17. DRAMAS (India)
18. INWARD (Australia)
19. ANIMAL (Philippines)
20. NERVED (USA)
21. ENCLAVE (France)
22. ANVIL (Lithuania)
23. TOKYO (Japan)
24. RACE (Israel)

Occupy Yourself**

Listed here are 25 different occupations and professions. Occupy yourself in a professional way by trying to unravel them.

1. GALORE
2. LEWDER
3. REWARD
4. THREAT
5. MARINA
6. RIOTED
7. STRIPE
8. RESIGN
9. RIALTO
10. CRANED
11. RETARD
12. STRAIT
13. CORKED
14. APRONS
15. WANDER
16. TROUT
17. MOANS
18. RUNES
19. DRIVE
20. BREAK
21. DREY
22. CASTERS
23. HECTARE
24. LAMINAR
25. STINTED

Gladstone***

The name of the British Prime Minister **WILLIAM EWART GLADSTONE** can be anagrammed into these relevant phrases:

> 1. Great wise old man, at will.
> 2. Go, administrate law well.
> 3. Wilt tear down all images.
> 4. Wild agitator means well.

Can you make at least four more phrases?

SOLUTIONS ON PAGE 348.

You Name It**

Here, in anagrammatic form, are the first names of boys and girls. Can you sort them out?

1. GEM	2. ROAD	3. LINE
4. SMILE	5. OSIER	6. HOARD
7. AURAL	8. GREAT	9. LETHE
10. GRADE	11. AMBLE	12. MAORI
13. IDEAL	14. LILAC	15. ASSET
16. SALLET	17. YONDER	18. DANGLE
19. SINGLY	20. ANTRIM	21. EVENTS
22. RIDING	23. HAMLET	24. EASTER

Problematic Phrases***

Each of the 18 phrases listed here can be turned into one single word. For example, the phrase **'Often sheds tears'** could become **'softheartedness'**. See if you can find the 18 words that make up these phrases – and the phrases should give you either a cryptic or a perverse clue to the words you are looking for.

For example, **IS NOT SOLACED** could lead you cryptically to **DISCONSOLATE** and **LET MAN LOVE** could lead you perversely to **MALEVOLENT**.

1. I HIRE PARSONS	2. REAL FUN
3. FINE TONIC	4. IT'S MORE FUN
5. SEEN AS MIST	6. TENDER NAMES
7. LET'S RUSH	8. A STEW, SIR?
9. OUR MEN EARN IT	10. NINE THUMPS
11. NICE LOVE	12. ILL FED
13. IS IT LEGAL? NO	14. I LIMIT ARMS
15. LIFE'S AIM	16. RESTORE PLUSH
17. A ROPE ENDS IT	18. GOT AS A CLUE

Presidential Poser**

AN ORAL DANGER is a phrase that can be rearranged to give the name of an American President. Which one?

SOLUTIONS ON PAGE 348.

One Over the Eight**

The sentence below was formed by rearranging the letters of a well known proverb. Which proverb?

THIS IS MEANT AS INCENTIVE

Prime Poser*

THAT GREAT CHARMER is a phrase that can be rearranged to give the name of another unique British Prime Minister. Which one?

SOLUTIONS ON PAGE 348.

HIDDEN WORDS

In the following puzzles you will find the given words hidden in the square. The words you have got to find may be written forwards or backwards, upwards or downwards or even diagonally.

Alpha Plus*

A is the only vowel you will find on this page. Can you find all 67 of the A words in the square opposite?

AARDVARK
ADAPT
ALMANAC
AMALGAM
ARRAS
AVATAR
BALD
BASALT
CABAL
CANAL
CANTATA
CASSAVA
CHARABANC
GALA
KRAAL
MADAGASCAR
MAHARAJA
MARSALA
PANDA
PHALANX
SALAAM
SAVANNA
VANDAL

ABRACADABRA
ALABAMA
ALPACA
ANAGRAM
ASP
BACCARAT
BANAL
BAZAAR
CALABASH
CANASTA
CARAVAN
CATAMARAN
DATA
GRANADA
LAVA
MADAM
MAHATMA
MASCARA
PARAGRAPH
RAMADAN
SALAD
TARMACADAM

ADAMANT
ALFALFA
ALTAR
ARMADA
ASTRAKHAN
BALACLAVA
BANANA
BWANA
CANADA
CANCAN
CASCARA
CATARACT
DRAMA
HALMA
LLAMA
MAGNA CARTA
MARACAS
PANAMA
PARALLAX
RATAPLAN
SARABAND
VALHALLA

```
A T P H A L A N X L A V A S S A C H A
A P N A L N T R A T L A A T S A N A C
S A V A N N A V A R A C M A S C A R A
A D M A L A D R V A L H A L L A B M C
J A K A B P M C A B A L D R A A A A A
A N R A G A A A L M A N A C N D R D N
R A A K C L S T C B A G M A A A A A T
A W V A V A A A A X A T N G C N H L A
H B D A A S L M L R Z A A S A K C V T
A A R V L R A A A T R S A C A D A A A
M L A A X A H G B A C C A R A T N H N
A A A N C M K N M A L C T M A S P A A
A M A D N A B A R A S S A R R A A L P
D L G A T A D C N F A H X T R C A M S
A L F L Z A S A G A A Z D G A A L A G
M R A A N A B R B T G J A R L R L T A
A S A A L A N T M R A R A P A A A G N
N R R A R F X A L L A R A P A M A C A
T G D A A K A C A P L A A M A Z A S T
```

SOLUTION ON PAGE 349.

X-Tract**

Extract the following words hidden in the diagram below.

ANNEX	APEX	APPENDIX	BORAX
BOX	CALX	CALYX	CICATRIX
CLIMAX	COAX	COCCYX	CODEX
COMPLEX	CORTEX	COX	CRUX
EQUINOX	FLAX	FLEX	FLUX
FOX	HELIX	HOAX	IBEX
ILEX	INDEX	KEX	LARYNX
LATEX	LYNX	MUREX	ONYX
ORYX	PARADOX	PAX	PHALANX
PHARYNX	PHLOX	PHOENIX	PREFIX
PYX	QUINCUNX	SEX	SPHINX
STYX	SUFFIX	SYNTAX	THORAX
VERTEX	VORTEX	WAX	

```
C X X Y H              X B I C X
O E X E L I           X O N A E X
D B L S T Y X        X R D L K I X
E I Q X X R X E    F A E X A F C Y
X E Q U I N O X T X X I N E O H P
  Y U L X V Y C E R R N R A X C
  X F C N O R X T E P X P X
  Y O W U R A X A V E W
  M M X C T H S L P
  T P X I D N E P P A X
 X H L C O P Y I X A H X H
  F L O E X L C S Y U N R I E X
X O A R X Y L A C U U Q A A N L P
X C R A N I X C  X F X U L D X F
O R Y X M A O    W F Q X A O H
B U N A L C      X I W M H X
X X X F X        X X E S P
```

Quoting the Bard***

You are asked to find in the diagram on page 213 the words which will complete the following quotations from Shakespeare, all of which have become part of everyday speech. Each missing word is denoted by a number of dashes representing the number of letters in the word.

If you are stumped by any of the quotations, a word list is on page 213.

1. '_ _ _ _ _ _ _ is such sweet sorrow' (ROMEO AND JULIET)

2. 'Sweet lovers love the _ _ _ _ _ _' (AS YOU LIKE IT)

3. 'I must be _ _ _ _ _, only to be kind' (HAMLET)

4. 'More sinned against than _ _ _ _ _ _ _' (KING LEAR)

5. 'A _ _ _ _ _ _ on both your houses' (ROMEO AND JULIET)

6. 'Though this be madness, yet there is _ _ _ _ _ _ in it' (HAMLET)

7. 'For this _ _ _ _ _ _ much thanks' (HAMLET)

8 'The time is out of _ _ _ _ _' (HAMLET)

9. 'There's a _ _ _ _ _ _ _ _ that shapes our ends' (HAMLET)

10. 'it did me yeoman's _ _ _ _ _ _ _' (HENRY IV PART i)

11. ''Twas _ _ _ _ _ _ _ to the general' (HAMLET)

12. 'When we have shuffled off this mortal _ _ _ _' (HAMLET)

13. 'For mine own part, it was _ _ _ _ _ to me' (JULIUS CAESAR)

14. 'The wheel is come full _ _ _ _ _ _' (KING LEAR)

15. '_ _ _ _ _ _ _ in stones' (AS YOU LIKE IT)

16. 'Sweet are the uses of _ _ _ _ _ _ _ _ _' (AS YOU LIKE IT)

17. 'I have not slept one _ _ _ _' ' (CYMBELINE)

18. '_ _ _ _ _ _ _ _ _ _ doth make cowards of us all' (HAMLET)

19. 'They come not single spies, but in _ _ _ _ _ _ _ _ _ _'
(HAMLET)

20. 'And thereby hangs a _ _ _ _' (AS YOU LIKE IT)

21. 'Well said; that was laid on with a _ _ _ _ _ _'
(AS YOU LIKE IT)

22. 'I could a tale _ _ _ _ _ _' (HAMLET)

23. 'A good deed in a _ _ _ _ _ _ _ world'
(THE MERCHANT OF VENICE)

24. 'The world's mine _ _ _ _ _ _'
(THE MERRY WIVES OF WINDSOR)

25. 'But I will wear my heart upon my _ _ _ _ _ _' (OTHELLO)

26. 'An _ _ _ _ _ _ _ _ _ _ _ thing, sir, but mine own'
(AS YOU LIKE IT)

27. 'Neither a _ _ _ _ _ _ _ _ nor a _ _ _ _ _ _ be' (HAMLET)

28. '_ _ _ _ _ _ _ is the soul of _ _ _' (HAMLET)

29. 'He hath eaten me out of _ _ _ _ _ and _ _ _ _'
(HENRY IV PART ii)

30. 'Thy _ _ _ _ was father, Harry, to the _ _ _ _ _ _ _'
(HENRY IV PART ii)

31. 'More in _ _ _ _ _ _ than in _ _ _ _ _' (HAMLET)

32. '_ _ _ _ _ _ and ministers of _ _ _ _ _ defend us' (HAMLET)

33. 'The _ _ _ _ _ _ of true _ _ _ _ never did run _ _ _ _ _ _'
(A MID-SUMMER NIGHT'S DREAM)

Parting	Spring	Cruel	Sinning
Plague	Method	Relief	Joint
Divinity	Service	Caviare	Coil
Greek	Circle	Sermons	Adversity
Wink	Conscience	Battalions	Tale
Trowel	Unfold	Naughty	Oyster
Sleeve	Ill-favoured	Borrower	Lender
Brevity	Wit	House	Home
Wish	Thought	Sorrow	Anger
Angels	Grace	Course	Love
Smooth			

```
T H I L V B E V O L B R U D T S G L E
F E I L E R M O V A G Y N A S R K Y S
U P V I L C O Y T I W H F N C H M B U
H T N E B F H T R V O D O H T E M T O
S T A B E R A I V A C M L O D H B E H
Y E O N O L J V I C R G D N W A R C T
T H E O I W S E O E V H A L O J I A B
J U C O M I T R S U G V I G R O G R Y
S K N I W S Y B O R R O W E R V E G B
D S E D T H D R G E E E K E O T J I O
I P I T T Y T I S R E V D A S D M N A
S R C C S M L O V Y K N A Y G L E I G
C I S P E Y H L L I E M O A N G E L S
R N N T R C T C E L N R E G N A S T O
E G O N V W I H C W D I V I Z C R A M
N T C H I R T H G U O H T O C R U E L
A L A Y C N O C L U Y R P Y F L O J I
J O O L E U G A L P A B T A A N C B O
H R E J E L I F I P T N I O J I N A C
```

Parlez-vous?**

You don't have to be French to find the following words in the diagram opposite:

A LA CARTE	AMOUR
APERITIF	ART NOUVEAU
AU REVOIR	AVOIRDUPOIS
BETE NOIRE	BIJOU
BISTRO	BONHOMIE
BON VIVEUR	BON VOYAGE
BOUILLON	BOURGEOIS
BOUTIQUE	CHAUFFEUR
CHEF	CHERCHEZ LA FEMME
COIFFEUR	COR ANGLAIS
CORDON BLEU	COUTURE
CROUTON	CUISINE
ENCORE	ENFANT TERRIBLE
ENNUI	ENTREE
ESPRIT DE CORPS	FAIT ACCOMPLI
FAUX PAS	GATEAU
GAUCHE	GRAND PRIX
HORS DE COMBAT	MAL DE MER
MASSEUR	MATINEE
NEGLIGEE	NOBLESSE OBLIGE
NOM DE PLUME	PIED-A-TERRE
ROTISSERIE	SAVOIR-FAIRE
VINGT-ET-UN	VIN ORDINAIRE

```
G R N C E V L C H A N G L E U Q I T U O B
R U N O L L I U O B A I R S T P U E L E Y
F E L I B G R N O R E V U A I R L E G I C
R F A U I L R U O M A R O E N B A A S H X
U F I O R E E E U R U N D I N D Y C E A O
E U A J R G E S P E D A G O R O P R A I S
V A H I E R O N S Y T I D L V D C R O L T
I H U B T W R S I E X R N N A H U C I F A
V C A N T A A I R T O S O A E I U P H X S
N F E C N M C R O C A B U Z I I S E O P Q
O L V O A V E C H V U M L Y S R O R R I U
B B U U F L U I O S E A T I E U E O S I S
E O O T N M G I R M F R N M G H C C D U A
T N N U E B R F F E P E U G H E T N E N P
E H T R R F L I M O S L E A D J O E C N X
N O R E A G T M O P P S I T E N G L O E U
O M A I D I E R U E F F I O C I A T M B A
I I R U R G L O D P I R C T L E U A B I F
R E M E D L A M I B P S H G O O C H A N G
E M P R A V O R T S I B E I R R H O T L E
D A R V I N G T E T U N F C U A E T A G O
```

SOLUTION ON PAGE 352.

The Haystack***

Can you find the word **NEEDLE**? It appears only once.

CIPHERS AND FRIENDS

What is the difference between a code and a cipher? Many people talk of 'secret codes' when they really mean 'secret ciphers'. Strictly speaking, a cipher is a system whereby every letter in the alphabet is replaced by another letter, number or symbol. A code is a system whereby one single word, letter or symbol can represent a whole sentence. Most of the following puzzles are designed to test your deciphering skills.

Two of a Kind**

Here are the names of two people we associate with a particular time of the year. Can you decipher their names?

     1. KFTVT DISJTU   2. TBOUB DMBVT

Film Fun**

The sequences of vowels and dashes below are the titles of various popular films. The consonants have been missed out, hence:
__E _A_ _E _E_E would be **THE WAY WE WERE**
Fill in the missing consonants.

  1. __E _OU__ O_ _U_L
  2. O_E __E_ O_E_ __E _U__OO_ _E__
  3. __E __E___ _IEU_E A___ _O_A_
  4. __A_ _A_
  5. _AU__A _L__ _E_E_
  6. E_L U__E_ __E _U_
  7. __A_IO__ O_ _LE
  8. _U_E__A
  9. A_LA_ _OU_E
10. _O_ _OU_ E_E_ O___

SOLUTIONS ON PAGE 353.

Word Numbers*

One cipher used by secret agents replaces letters with numbers. In a simple version of this **A** becomes **1**, **B** becomes **2**, and so on, with **Z** being **26**. The following words are in a number cipher, but **A** is **3**, **B** is **4**, and so on. Can you decipher the words?

1. 20 7 5 22 11 8 27
2. 18 3 22 20 11 3 20 5 10
3. 10 7 20 3 14 6
4. 9 20 17 22 7 21 19 23 7
5. 24 7 16 22 11 14 3 22 7
6. 22 20 7 15 23 14 17 23 21
7. 21 16 11 9 9 7 20
8. 20 7 23 16 11 17 16
9. 18 20 17 22 7 11 16
10. 15 17 16 21 22 20 17 23 21
11. 14 23 15 11 16 3 20 27
12. 11 6 11 17 21 27 16 5 20 3 21 27
13. 8 20 23 21 22 20 3 22 7
14. 6 20 3 23 9 10 22 21 15 3 16
15. 6 11 21 22 3 16 5 7

Novel Quiz**

These ten book titles are written without any vowels. Can you insert vowels amongst the consonants to form the titles **and** name the author of the work in each instance?

1. BLK HS
2. NNTN GHTY FR
3. MM
4. JN YR
5. WNN TH PH
6. PRSSN
7. TH TL F PTR RBBT
8. FRM RSS WTH LV
9. FRNKNSTN
10. LTTL WMN

SOLUTIONS ON PAGE 354.

Sounds Familiar*

These letters represent a conversation that took place recently in an East European hotel between two secret agents. One was posing as a waiter, the other was ordering breakfast. Both spoke in English, but with unusual accents. What did they say?

```
F  U  N  E  X  ?

S  V  F  X

F  U  N  E  M  ?

S  V  F  M

O  K  L  F  M  N  X
```

Mixed Faith***

The following jumbled quotations are all taken from the Bible. Can you rearrange them to read their original meaning?

1. Thou servant good and well, faithful done.
   (St Matthew Ch. 25 v. 23)

2. Over his love was me banner.
   (Song of Solomon Ch. 2 v. 4)

3. Am am I I that.
   (Exodus Ch. 3 v. 14)

4. Escaped I am with the teeth skin of my.
   (Job Ch. 19 v. 20)

SOLUTIONS ON PAGE 354.

5. But a sword came I not to send peace.
(St Matthew Ch. 10 v. 34)

6. Hear hear that let ears to him hath he.
(St Mark Ch. 4. v. 9)

7. Not him received own his and own his unto came he.
(St John Ch. 1 v. 11)

8. In hope believed hope against who.
(Romans Ch. 4 v. 18)

9. I I have have written written what.
(St John Ch. 19 v. 22)

10. Yea nay yea nay and let your your be.
(James Ch. 5 v. 12)

11. After his own heart a man.
(1 Samuel Ch. 13 v. 14)

False Start*

Can you understand this message?

GALLB GTHEY RFIRSTQ

HANDX TALLY STHEJ
KLASTH YLETTERSN

WARET PFALSEM

Vowel Play**

In ye olden days people were encouraged to keep the ten commandments by learning this rhyming couplet. Add the same missing vowel in the appropriate places and see if you can make sense of the couplet today.

PRSVR Y PRFCT MN

VR KP THS PRCPTS TN

Unnatural Break*

What does this message say?

AL LOU RLIV ESWEA RECRU SHE DBYTHEWEI GHTOFW ORDS

Alphabetical Extractions***

The words below have each had a different letter removed wherever it occurs in the word. One word has had two or more A's extracted, one word has had two or more B's extracted, and so on through the alphabet. Thus FLUFFY might appear as LUY. Can you discover the 26 original words.

1. VRGRN	2. RYTM	3. INIU	4. UINUIREME
5. NGRM	6. IETEE	7. ARLIN	8. IGAM
9. YLI	10. UIES	11. INY	12. GPS
13. UCCE	14. ERES	15. HIRY	16. ANARE
17. EASIE	18. SUUR	19. HOO	20. IABE
21. JAY	22. AMNE	23. LLATE	24. EUNE
25. VD	26. RONC		

The Word***

Here is an English word with ecclesiastical associations. It isn't very common, but if you know your Roman numerals you should find it easy. It can be found in any dictionary.

E10100010001000UNI100ATXN

Full Marx*

What do you need to make sense of these letters? Movie buffs will love this puzzle.

1. NML CRCKRS 2. MNKY BSNSS 3. HRS FTHRS
4. DCK SP 5. NGHT T TH PR 6. DY T TH RCS

WHAT OCCURS ONCE IN A MINUTE, TWICE IN A MOMENT, BUT NOT ONCE IN A HUNDRED YEARS?

THE LETTER M.

SOLUTIONS ON PAGES 354 AND 355.

WORD CIRCLES AND LADDERS AND SQUARES

Word Circles***

Each circle of letters makes up a familiar eight letter word, written in either a clockwise or an anticlockwise direction. Identify all 16 words as quickly as you can.

1.
```
    R
  C   E
  I   O
  O   C
    N
```

2.
```
    T
  A   I
  I   C
  C   C
    S
```

3.
```
    E
  M   N
  A   C
  L   Y
    C
```

4.
```
    E
  V   R
  E   B
  I   E
    L
```

5.
```
    E
  M   S
  O   Y
  R   N
    D
```

6.
```
    E
  R   D
  O   U
  T   C
    A
```

7.
```
    O
  R   L
  I   A
  G   N
    I
```

8.
```
    S
  T   Y
  E   H
  R   C
    I
```

9.
```
    M
  R   O
  A   N
  H   I
    C
```

10.
```
    L
  E   Y
  G   O
  A   G
    R
```

11.
```
    I
  C   T
  A   S
  L   Y
    M
```

12.
```
    H
  A   A
  C   D
  I   N
    E
```

13.
```
    N
  E   M
  M   C
  O   I
    N
```

14.
```
    T
  E   E
  M   M
  R   R
    O
```

15.
```
    N
  A   I
  P   R
  H   E
    C
```

16.
```
    O
  G   L
  L   U
  Y   E
    S
    T
```

Magic Spell***

One of the best-known 'magic' words must be **ABRACADABRA**. In centuries gone by the word was used as a magic charm to ward off evil spirits. The word would be written on parchment and hung around the neck. A popular way of writing the charm was like this:

```
        A
       B B
      R R R
     A A A A
    C C C C C
   A A A A A A
  D D D D D D D
 A A A A A A A A
B B B B B B B B B
R R R R R R R R R R
A A A A A A A A A A A
```

See if you can count the number of ways it is possible to spell out the word **ABRACADABRA** on such an amulet, by starting from the A at the top and always proceeding from one letter to an adjacent one. You can move diagonally to the left or right and change direction after each letter.

SOLUTION ON PAGE 355.

Six-Letter Odd-Ends**

Here are 42 familiar six-letter words with uncommon endings. Can you supply the missing letters to complete the words?

1. _ _ _ ODA	2. _ _ _ HMA	3. _ _ _ RUB
4. _ _ _ HID	5. _ _ _ IOD	6. _ _ _ URD
7. _ _ _ EXE	8. _ _ _ ALF	9. _ _ _ ULF
10. _ _ _ ZOI	11. _ _ _ GEL	12. _ _ _ FIL
13. _ _ _ SUL	14. _ _ _ THM	15. _ _ _ TIM
16. _ _ _ HOM	17. _ _ _ XEN	18. _ _ _ EMN
19. _ _ _ EBO	20. _ _ _ CCO	21. _ _ _ OCO
22. _ _ _ REO	23. _ _ _ DIO	24. _ _ _ AMO
25. _ _ _ KOO	26. _ _ _ RYO	27. _ _ _ AAR
28. _ _ _ UAR	29. _ _ _ EOR	30. _ _ _ UOR
31. _ _ _ HYR	32. _ _ _ VAS	33. _ _ _ GIS
34. _ _ _ GAT	35. _ _ _ IAT	36. _ _ _ VAT
37. _ _ _ DAU	38. _ _ _ OLU	39. _ _ _ VEX
40. _ _ _ AXY	41. _ _ _ NTZ	42. _ _ _ RTZ

Bird Fivers*

Take a letter from each bird in turn to spell another 5-letter bird.

```
F   I   N   C   H

G   R   E   B   E

E   A   G   L   E

S   N   I   P   E

H   E   R   O   N
```

In for a Spell**

The word square below is made up of 25 letters of the alphabet, omitting the letter Q. Start at any of the letters and moving one letter at a time (up, down, right, left, or diagonally) see how many different words you can spell out. Do not use any letter more than once in the same word. You can change direction after each letter. All words must be of at least three letters, and no proper names, plurals, abbreviations or foreign words can be used. Aim for a minimum of 20 words.

```
A   B   C   D   E

J   I   H   G   F

K   L   M   N   O

U   T   S   R   P

V   W   X   Y   Z
```

Musical Spell***

In the network below the names of 14 musical instruments are hidden. To spell out the instruments you can start from any letter, and the consecutive letters of the word will be contained in adjacent cells connected horizontally, vertically or diagonally.

```
F   I   N   V   O

L   E   P   I   L

U   T   R   M   A

A   B   U   D   N

M   O   E   G   O
```

Fill-ins**

With this puzzle all you have to do is fill in the blanks__ and to help you, in each puzzle, it's the same letters that are missing from each line. Here's an example:

```
T __
_ T _
__ T
```

All you've got to do is think of the two letters that are missing from each line and, when you've thought of them, fill them in. Since abbreviations aren't allowed it won't take you long to realise that **E** and **A** are the missing letters in the example and that, filled in, the puzzle looks like this:

> **TEA**
>
> **ATE**
>
> **EAT**

Here's another, more difficult one:

> _ _ P
>
> _ P _
>
> P _ _

The missing letters are **T** and **A**, so it looks like this:

> **TAP**
>
> **APT**
>
> **PAT**

Now you've got the idea, see how you get on with these:

1. R _ _
  _ R _
  _ _ R

2. S _ _ S
  _ S _ S
  _ _ S S
  S _ _ S

3. C _ _ _ S
  S C _ _ _
  _ _ C _ S

4. R I _ _ _ _
  _ R I _ _ _
  _ _ R I _ _

5. _ _ A M _
  _ _ _ A M
  M _ A _ _
  M A _ _ _
  _ A M _ _

6. P _ _ T
  P _ T _
  T _ P _
  _ T _ P
  _ P _ T

7. _ O O _
  _ O _ O
  _ O O _

8. _ E _ D
  D _ _ E
  _ _ D E

SOLUTIONS ON PAGE 355.

Word Ladders***

Lewis Carroll introduced us to Word Ladders. The idea is a simple one. For example, you might be asked to change APE into MAN by altering one letter at a time, without altering the position of the other letters, and always leaving a true word as the link word:

APE
APT
OPT
OAT
MAT
MAN

Here are some of the best of Lewis Carroll's own Word Ladder challenges:

1. Drive **PIG** into **STY** with four links.

2. Raise **FOUR** to **FIVE** with six links.

3. Make **WHEAT** into **BREAD** with six links.

4. Touch **NOSE** with **CHIN** with five links.

5. Change **TEARS** INTO **SMILE** with five links.

6. Make **HARE** into **SOUP** with six links.

7. **PITCH TENTS** with five links.

8. Cover **EYE** with **LID** with three links.

9. Prove **PITY** to be **GOOD** with six links.

10. Turn **POOR** into **RICH** with five links.

11. Get **WOOD** from **TREE** with seven links.

12. Prove **GRASS** to be **GREEN** with seven links.

13. Make **FLOUR** into **BREAD** with five links.

14. Make **TEA HOT** with three links.

15. Get **COAL** from **MINE** with five links.

16. Change **BLACK** to **WHITE** with six links.

17. Turn **WITCH** into **FAIRY** with 12 links.

18. Make **WINTER SUMMER** with 13 links.

SOLUTIONS ON PAGE 356.

INTERNATIONAL WORDWAYS

Ici Français**

There are many French words and phrases that have almost become part of everyday English. Here are a few. Do you know what they mean?

1. A bientôt
2. Adieu
3. Affair de coeur
4. Aide de camp
5. A la mode
6. Au fait
7. Avant garde
8. Bijou
9. Billet doux
10. Blasé
11. Cartouche
12. Chacun à son gôut
13. Coup de grâce
14. Décolletage
15. Déjà vu
16. Mot juste
17. Nom de guerre
18. Outré
19. Passé
20. Risqué

HOW CAN YOU SAY 'I AM LOOKING FOR YOU' IN 3 LETTERS?

SOLUTIONS ON PAGE 357.

Hidden Countries**

The names of two countries are hidden in each of the ten sentences below. Can you discover them? For instance, in the sentence 'Interpol and the FBI discover hidden marksmen', **POLAND** is concealed in the first two words and **DENMARK** is concealed in the last two words.

1. Vladimir and Olga are Soviet names.

2. Have you ever heard an animal talk in dialect?

3. In letters to the press we denounce the wholesale ban on luxury imports.

4. Evening classes may help an amateur to improve his painting.

5. Children put on galoshes to go out in the rain.

6. Rash decisions may cause trouble so thorough analysis is a necessity.

7. The viscount has not found a home yet and he regrets leaving his fine palace.

8. If your exhaust pipe rusts you just have to shrug and accept it.

9. Such a display could be either grand or rather vulgar.

10. Give the dog a bone and give him a little water.

Origins***

The following words can be found in any English dictionary, but from which languages did they originate?

1. Pince nez	2. Cul de sac	3. Pro tempore
4. Mañana	5. Fait accompli	6. Allegro
7. Bona fide	8. Mufti	9. Nosh
10. Pagoda	11. Voodoo	12. Taboo
13. Ombudsman	14. Origami	15. Guru
16. Kismet	17. Pundit	18. Quisling
19. Swastika	20. Halcyon	21. Habeas corpus
22. Marathon	23. Colossal	24. Vigilante

SOLUTIONS ON PAGE 357.

Slang Words*

In Cockney rhyming slang, the rhyming part is often omitted. For example, titfer (tit for tat, in full) is hat, and plates (plates of meat) are feet. Can you join each of the words in the first column to its rhyming part in the second column, and find its meaning in the third column? For example, apples (from the first column) and pears (from the second column) means stairs (from the third column).

WHISTLE	VARDEN	WIFE
TROUBLE	ROOTS	TEA
ROSIE	PLATE	SUIT
PIG'S	LEE	STAIRS
DOLLY	HOOK	MONEY
DAISY	EAR	MATE
CHINA	AND STRIFE	LOOK
BUTCHER'S	AND HONEY	GARDEN
BEES	AND PEARS	BOOTS
APPLES	AND FLUTE	BEER

English Spoken Here**

Below are some English words and phrases. Can you give the French equivalent? They are probably more familiar than the English.

1. According to the menu
2. With reference to
3. Trinket
4. Enjoy your meal
5. A witty comment
6. Miscellaneous objects
7. Complete freedom
8. That's life!
9. Exclusive group
10. Announcer at a revue
11. Habitual flirt
12. The best people
13. First performance
14. Social blunder
15. Style
16. Medley or mixture
17. Sharp, stinging
18. Powerful exhibition of skill
19. With regard to
20. Grand gesture

SOLUTIONS ON PAGE 357.

Down Under**

Australians speak English, but the English they speak isn't always exactly the same English as the English speak. When you are Down Under you may meet a banana bender and you will find he's got nothing to do with bananas: he just happens to come from Queensland. And if his first words to you are **'Don't come the raw prawn!'** he's not talking about uncooked shrimps, he is simply saying **'You can't fool me!'**

To find out if you would be fooled by an Australian speaking Australian, take a look at this list of Down Under English words and see how many you can match with the British equivalent in the second column.

Aussie	Sweets
Bathers	Mate
Billabong	Countryside
Bowser	Australian wild dog
Bush (the)	Sheep
Cobber	Baby kangaroo
Didgeridoo	Pupil on sheep/cattle station
Dingo	Bundle of belongings
Dinkum	Postman
Duds	Small wallaby
Goanna	Idiot
Good on you	Australia/Australian
Grazier	Petrol Pump
Gum tree	Suitcase
Jackeroo	Shark
Joey	Farmer
Jumbuck	Well done!
Lollies	Girl/woman
Milk bar	Eucalyptus tree
Moke	Lizard
Noah's ark	Pond
Nong	Swimming costume
Paddy melon	Trumpet
Pommy	Honest
Port	Englishman/woman
Postie	Horse
Sheila	Best clothes
Swag	Dairy & general grocery shop

SOLUTIONS ON PAGE 358.

PICTURE PUZZLES

SECTION ONE

Spot the Difference 1. Shop!*

This puzzle features two seemingly identical pictures, A and B. Whereas, in fact, picture B contains a dozen distinct differences. Can you spot them?

SOLUTION ON PAGE 359.

Maze 1*

Spot the Mistake 1. Bonjour!*

'I do not mind lying, but I hate inaccuracy,' said Samuel Butler, and the truth is that in the following two drawings there may be one or two (or even three) inaccuracies. The Eiffel Tower sets the scene in France. Can you spot them?

SOLUTION ON PAGE 359.

Spot the Mistake 2. Cor Blimey!*

Something to shout about the day after the Coronation.

SOLUTION ON PAGE 359.

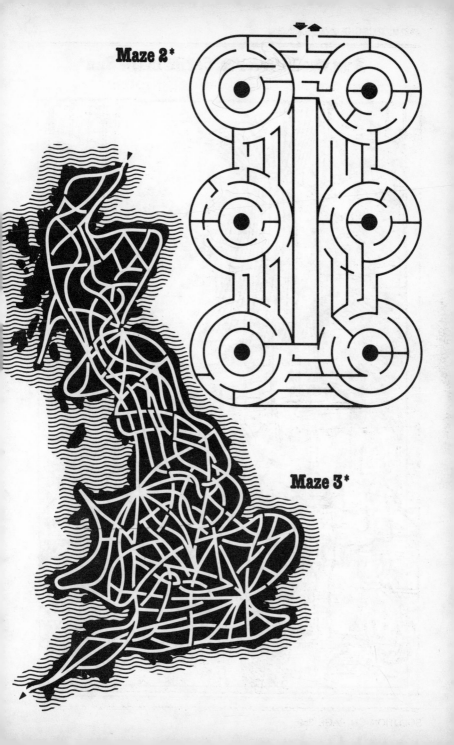

Maze 2*

Maze 3*

Spot the Difference 2. Fun in the Sun*

Picture B contains a dozen differences from picture A. Can you spot them?

NUMBER PUZZLES

NUMBER FUN

Twenty Questions**

Here's a quick quiz in which all the questions have something to do with numbers. Otherwise the questions have nothing in common, they range from literary subjects, through films to baked beans! However, in order to jog your memory each question has four possible answers from which you have to choose the right one.

1. Is **'Number 10'** –
   (a) the name of a make of cigarette?
   (b) the name of an expensive perfume?
   (c) the address of the British Prime Minister?
   (d) the name of a secret society?

2. Is a **'747'** –
   (a) a kind of germ?
   (b) a kind of shotgun?
   (c) a kind of bomb?
   (d) a kind of aeroplane?

3. Who wrote **The Thirty-nine Steps?** Was it –
   (a) Agatha Christie?
   (b) Arthur Conan Doyle?
   (c) John Buchan?
   (d) John Galsworthy?

4. **4,406 feet** represents the height of which famous mountain –
   (a) Ben Nevis?
   (b) Mont Blanc?
   (c) Mount Everest?
   (d) Mount Pico?

5. Who boasts about having **'57 Varieties'**? Is it –
   (a) Rolls-Royce who make motor cars?
   (b) Rowntrees who make sweets?
   (c) Heinz who make tinned foods?
   (d) Waddingtons who make games?

SOLUTIONS ON PAGE 362.

6. Who wrote a novel called **1984**? Was it –
   - (a) George Washington?
   - (b) George Orwell?
   - (c) George Brown?
   - (d) George III?

7. What is or was the only coin in the world with **7 sides**? Is it, or was it –
   - (a) the old French 10 franc piece?
   - (b) the new British 20p piece?
   - (c) the German Deutschmark?
   - (d) the British 50p piece?

8. If you multiply **9** by **99** and multiply the result by **999** what do you get. Is it –

   - (a) 999,999?
   - (b) 890,109?
   - (c) 9,999,999?
   - (d) 4,765,220?

9. What is or was **2001**? Is it or was it –
   - (a) the name of a new brand of toothpaste?
   - (b) the name of a famous railway train?
   - (c) the name of a well-known shoe polish?
   - (d) the name of a science-fiction novel and film?

10. Who created **Special Agent 007**? Was it –
    - (a) John Le Carré?
    - (b) John Le Mesurier?
    - (c) Ian Fleming?
    - (d) Ian Carmichael?

11. Which was the first of the **Seven Wonders of the World**. Was it –
    - (a) The Pyramids of Egypt?
    - (b) The Taj Mahal?
    - (c) The Grand Canyon?
    - (d) The Eiffel Tower?

12. Were the **Seven Samurai** –
    - (a) Indian temples?

SOLUTIONS ON PAGE 362.

(b) Chinese Sweets?
(c) African weapons?
(d) Japanese Warriors?

13. In the Bible story, to whom did God give the **Ten Commandments** –
(a) Solomon?
(b) David?
(c) Jesus?
(d) Moses?

14. 2.540 centimetres is the same as –
(a) ¼ inch?
(b) 1 inch?
(c) 6 inches?
(d) 2 feet?

15. What was the **R101**? Was it –
(a) a type of submarine?
(b) a type of airship?
(c) a type of steam engine?
(d) a type of motor cycle?

16. Who wrote the book **Around the World in Eighty Days** from which the film was made? Was it –
(a) H.G. Wells?
(b) Jules Verne?
(c) Hammond Innes?
(d) Georges Simenon?

17. According to the song, how many trombones were there in the big parade –
(a) 2?
(b) 51?
(c) 76?
(d) 110?

18. If you multiply **2** times **2** times **2** times **2** times **2** times **2** times **2** times **2** times **2** times **2**, what do you get? Is it –
(a) 2,222,222?
(b) 2,000?
(c) 864?
(d) 1,024?

SOLUTIONS ON PAGE 362.

19. With what game do you associate the phrases 'Legs 11', 'All the fours, 44' and 'On its own, number 1'? Is it –
    (a) Cricket?
    (b) Bingo?
    (c) Roulette?
    (d) Bowls?

20. **8.047 kilometres** are the same as –
    (a) 10 miles?
    (b) 8 miles?
    (c) 5 miles?
    (d) 1 mile?

What Next**

In this series of numbers, what number comes next:

$$1\ 2\ 3\ 4\ 5\ 6\ 7\ 8\ -\ ?$$

Did you say 9? Quite right. Well done. Let's make it a little tougher now. In this series, what comes next:

  a. 3 3 4 4 5 5 6 – ?
  b. T T T F F S S E – ?
  c. 3 4 6 7 9 10 12 13 – ?
  d. 1 9 1 4 1 9 1 8 1 9 3 9 1 9 4 – ?
  e. 99 86 83 70 67 54 51 38 – ?
  f. O T T F F S S E N – ?
  g. 10 15 13 18 16 21 19 24 22 – ?
  h. 4445 7 89512 56734 42 89612 57 90 – ?

Pick a Number**

1. In Europe a **BILLION** equals a million times a million: 1,000,000,000,000. In America a billion's rather different. What does the American billion look like?

1,000,000,000?

1,000,000,000,000,000?

1,000,000,000,000,000,000,000?

1,000,000,000,000,000,000,000,000,000?

Pick a number

SOLUTIONS ON PAGE 362.

2. The Amazon is the world's longest river. How long is it?

2,899 miles?

4,195 miles?

6,800 miles?

12,631 miles?

Pick a number.

3. In the world today, there are roughly three babies born every second. In round figures, how many babies are born in a year?

60,000,000?

90,000,000?

120,000,000?

117,000,000,000?

Pick a number.

4. If a hippopotamus lived as long as it is possible for a hippopotamus to live, how old would the hippo be when he died?

10?

20?

40?

100?

Pick a number.

5. English is the second most spoken language in the world. How many people speak it?

291,000,000?

500,000,000?

994,000,000?

12,872,000,000?

Pick a number.

SOLUTIONS ON PAGE 362.

6. There are approximately two and a half centimetres in an inch, how many kilometres are there in a mile?

0.8?

1.6093?

2?

2.9802?

Pick a number

7. There are several theories about how the earth was formed but how old is it reckoned to be?

4,700,000,000 years?

4,700,000,000,000 years?

4,700,000,000,000,000 years?

4,700,000,000,000,000,000 years?

Pick a number.

8. If the capacity of a bus is around 50 cubic metres, what would you expect the capacity of a village church to be?

$100 \, m^3$?

$1,000 \, m^3$?

$10,000 \, m^3$?

$100,000 \, m^3$?

Pick a number.

9. A European **trillion** equals a million times a billion, so what does a European trillion look like?

1,000,000,000,000?

1,000,000,000,000,000?

1,000,000,000,000,000,000?

1,000,000,000,000,000,000,000?

Pick a number.

SOLUTIONS ON PAGE 362.

10. The tallest tree in Britain is a Grand Fir at Leighton Park in Gwent (Wales). How tall is it?

> 20 m?
> 38 m?
> 56 m?
> 72 m?

Pick a number.

Punch and Judy**

If you add the age of Punch to the age of Judy you get a combined age of 91 years. Punch is now twice as old as Judy was when he was as old as she is now. How old are Punch and Judy?

Monday to Friday**

Lady Agatha, when asked her age, replied that she was 35 years old, not counting Saturdays and Sundays. What was her real age?

AD/BC*

A man was born in the year 50 BC. How old was he on his birthday in 50 AD?

Next Please**

In each of these series what should the next number be?

1. 31 28 31 30 —

2. 3 6 12 24 –

3. 1 8 3 7 1 9 0 –

4. 2 3 5 9 17 33 –

5. 5 5 25 8 8 64 3 3 –

6. 1 12 1 1 1 2 1 3 –

7. 1 6 2 7 3 8 4 –

8. 940 839 738 637 –

9. 4 8 32 512 131072 –

10. 111.11111 125 142.85714 166.66666 200 –

Big Shot*

Johnny, Willy and Bobby were fishing by the river, when suddenly someone on the other bank fired a gun. Johnny saw the smoke rising from the gun, Willy saw the bullet hit the water with a splash, and Bobby heard the gun go off with a loud bang. Which of the three boys knew about the shot first?

Now What?*

What should come next in this series? And why?

½ 1 2 5 10 20 50 1 5 10

How Much**

How much money would I have originally had in my wallet, if in spending one-fifth and then one-fifth of what remained, I altogether spent £36.00 somewhere?

SOLUTIONS ON PAGES 362 AND 363.

Where There's a Will***

Mr Brown died recently, and in his will left just over £8,000 to be divided between his widow, his 5 sons, and 4 daughters. He stipulated that every son should receive three times as much as a daughter, and that every daughter should receive twice as much as their mother. If the precise amount left by the man was £8,000.07 how much did the widow receive?

Not so Silly Willy***

At the beginning of January little Willie told his parents that he had decided to save all his pocket money. He knew that he had been spending far too much and he realised that the time had come to put by some of the money his parents gave him for a rainy day. This was his plan:

On the first day of the month he wanted to save 1 penny.

On the second day of the month he wanted to save twice as much, two pennies.

On the third day of the month he wanted to save twice as much again, 4 pennies.

On the fourth day of the month he wanted to save twice as much again, 8 pennies.

On the fifth day he wanted to save twice as much again, 16 pennies.

And so he went on right through the month, each day saving twice as much as he'd saved the day before. Little Willie's parents, being sensible people, decided to encourage his thrift and gave him all the money he needed.

How much had little Willie managed to save by the last day of January?

Drink Up*

Two fathers and two sons went into an hotel to have a drink. The bill came to a total of £3. They each spent the same amount. How much did they pay?

The Lost Note**

Three men went into an hotel and were told that only one room was available and that it would cost £30 for the night. They each paid £10 and went to the room. Later that evening the receptionist realised that she had made an error and had overcharged the men £5. She asked one of the other hotel staff to return the £5 to the men. Unfortunately, this employee was none too honest. He realised that, since £5 is not easily divisible by 3, he would keep £2 and return £3 to the men so that each would get back £1. Each man therefore only paid £9, which totals £27 for the room. Add to that the £2 the employee kept, and the total is only £29.

What happened to the missing £1? Who had it? Where did it go?

Share Out**

You have three boys, Alex, Bobby and Colin. Divide 4,700 pennies among the three boys so that Alex gets 1,000 more pennies than Bobby, and Bobby receives 800 pennies more than Colin. How many pennies does each boy receive?

Bow and Arrow*

A bow and arrow cost £21. The bow costs £20 more than the arrow.
What is the price of each?

The Pools Winner***

Lucky had a win on the pools. On the day he collected his winnings he spent 95p. The next day he spent £1.90. The next day £2.85. The day after that £3.80, and so on, each day spending 95p more than on the previous day until finally he spent the last £190 of his winnings buying drinks for all his friends in the local pub.

What did Lucky's total winnings amount to?

WHAT TIME IS IT WHEN THE CLOCK STRIKES THIRTEEN?

TIME TO GET A NEW CLOCK.

SOLUTIONS ON PAGE 363.

Auntie Nellie***

Auntie Nellie decided to leave £1,000 amongst her 5 nieces, but her last will and testament specified that the girls had to divide the money according to their ages, so that each niece received £20 more than the next niece younger to her.

How much did the youngest of the five nieces receive?

See a Man About a Dog**

A farmer bought a sheepdog, only to find that it was frightened of sheep. Fortunately for him some American tourists visited his farm and fell in love with the animal. As they cared little about its sheepishness, he sold the dog to them for £35 and half as much as he gave for it. The tourists were happy with their purchase, and the farmer had made a profit of £10.50.

How much did the farmer originally pay for the dog?

A Pound of Apples*

Two market traders were selling apples. One was selling 30 apples for £1, whilst the other offered 20 apples for £1. One afternoon they were both called away, and each had 300 apples unsold. These they handed to a friend to sell at 50 for £2.

It will be seen that if they had sold their apples separately, they would have made £25, but when they were sold together, they fetched only £24.

So what has happened to the missing pound? Surely, 30 for £1 and 20 for £1 is the same as 50 for £2, isn't it?

Inflation***

During the 4 years of my membership, my annual subscriptions to the F.A.I.L. (the Federated Anti-Inflation League) totalled £120. In the second year the subscription was £3 more than in the first year; in the third it was £2 more than in the second; and in the fourth year £6 more than in the third.

How much was the subscription for each year?

Your Number's Up*

In a local do-it-yourself shop, my neighbour was quoted 12 pence for one, 24 pence for 50, and 36 pence for 144. He wanted 6.

What was he buying and how much did it cost him?

Muggers' Money***

Two English gentlemen, Mr Ascot and Mr Berkshire, with £100 and £48 respectively, having to perform a journey through a lonely part of the country, decided to travel together for purposes of company. As they were walking through a wood a gang of youths jumped out and threatened them. The gang leader was satisfied with taking twice as much from Mr Ascot as from Mr Berkshire and left to Mr Ascot three times as much as to Mr Berkshire.

How much was taken from each?

Long Time*

A woman wound up two watches. It turned out that one of them went two minutes per hour too slow, and the other went one minute per hour too fast. When she looked at them again, the faster one was exactly one hour ahead of the other.

How long had the watches been running.

On Strike**

If an ordinary striking clock was turned into a 24 hour clock, so that at midnight it struck 24 times, how many times would the clock strike in a full 24 hour day?

Long Hands**

On a clock with an hour hand and a minute hand of the same length and indistinguishable, if the clock were set going at noon, what would be the first time that it would be impossible, by reason of the similarity of the hands, to be certain of the correct time? To give an exact answer you may need to deal in fractions of a second.´

Felines and Rodents**

If 6 cats can devour 6 rats in one-tenth of an hour, how many would it take to devour 100 rats in 6,000 seconds?

SOLUTIONS ON PAGES 363 AND 364.

Stitches in Time**

If two stitchers can stitch two stitches in two seconds, how many stitches can six stitchers stitch in six seconds?

Timetable***

A man was in a great hurry to catch the 1.15 pm train from Liverpool Street, and it was already past 1 o'clock. In the distance he saw a church clock, and although he could not see the dial he could just distinguish that the two hands were exactly together, so he knew what the time must be.

What was the time?

Party Time***

At a late night party it appeared to the guests that the clock had stopped half way through the party because the hands appeared in exactly the same position as when the party began. In fact the hands had actually changed places. As the party began between 10 and 11 o'clock, what were the two times?

Digital Clock*

What should be the next number in the sequence?

1 2 5 9 5 8 1 2 5 9 5 9 1 3 . . .

The 'magic' of the Magic Square lies in the fact that whichever way you add up the numbers in the square – vertically, horizontally or diagonally – you always get the same answer. In this square, for example, the answer is always 15:

```
8 1 6
3 5 7
4 9 2
```

Here is another square, where the total for each line adds up to 62:

23	10	9	20
12	17	18	15
16	13	14	19
11	22	21	8

In this third sixteen-number square, the total is 150:

45	32	31	42
34	39	40	37
38	35	36	41
33	44	43	30

This next magic square contains twenty-five numbers. They add up to 105 in each direction, and if you add the four corner squares to the square in the middle you get 105 yet again:

25	32	9	16	23
31	13	15	22	24
12	14	21	28	30
18	20	27	29	11
19	26	33	10	17

Quarter of a Century***

The square below contains the numbers 1 to 25, and as you will see, all the rows, columns and long diagonals add up to 65.

17	24	1	8	15
23	5	7	14	16
4	6	13	20	22
10	12	19	21	3
11	18	25	4	9

What you have to do is try and form a similar Magic Square, using all the numbers 1 to 25, but begin with the number 1 in the centre of your square. The rows, columns, and diagonals must all add up to 65.

SOLUTIONS ON PAGE 364.

Radioactive Problem***

Nuclear waste is always a problem. If too much radioactive material is put together it is liable to endanger any living object within quite a wide range. Some radioactive materials, such as uranium, are kept in canisters and are buried in the ground. The diagram below represents 9 such canisters, each with a number on the top to show the strength of the material contained within.

This particular group, however, is highly dangerous because if 3 canisters are in a row their total strength must not be more than thirty units. If you add up the rows you will see that in many cases the totals far exceed the recommended safety limit.

$$13 \quad 6 \quad 14$$
$$11 \quad 10 \quad 3$$
$$9 \quad 17 \quad 7$$

Can you rearrange the containers so that no single line (row, column or diagonal) adds up to more than thirty? Owing to the possible risk to your health, make sure you move the smallest number of containers you can.

Nine-a-side**

Lord Crabtree bought 28 bottles of wine, and not sure whether he could trust the butler, he placed the bottles in his cellar in a container, in such a way that he could count 9 bottles on each side, like this:

$$2 \quad 5 \quad 2$$
$$5 \qquad 5$$
$$2 \quad 5 \quad 2$$

Notwithstanding this precaution, the butler removed 4 bottles and rearranged the bottles so that the next time Lord Crabtree counted them there were still 9 bottles on each side. Delighted by his cunning, the butler removed a further 4 bottles on the following day, and again rearranged the bottles so as to count 9 bottles along each side. How did he do it?

Misplacement*

In the Magic Square below all the lines of four figures should add up to 34, whether read across, down or diagonally. By mistake, two numbers have been wrongly placed. Can you discover which two?

16	3	2	13
5	10	11	8
9	6	12	7
4	15	14	1

Amazing!**

Here is a remarkable magic square. Work out whether or not the rows, columns and diagonals all total the same, and what that total is. Then decide what is the special property of this particular square?

8818	1111	8188	1881
8181	1888	8811	1118
1811	8118	1181	8888
1188	8881	1818	8111

CALCULATOR PUZZLES

If mental arithmetic is not to your liking, you many prefer push button puzzles. For these calculating brainteasers are for you; all you need is a pocket calculator. The solutions are then at your fingertips.

SOLUTIONS ON PAGE 364.

Mini Quiz*

This is a quiz and calculation combined:

1. Multiply the year of the Battle of Waterloo by a score.
2. Multiply the answer by the number of days in May.
3. Divide the answer by the number of years in a decade.
4. Add one percent of an American billion.
5. Now subtract the date of the Battle of Trafalgar.
6. Divide the total by the number of years an octogenarian has lived.

What is the answer?

Talking Calculators*

Incredible as it may sound, pocket calculators have names. To find out the name of yours, press 317537 and turn the calculator upside down.

Now that you see your calculator can spell as well as calculate, what numbers would you need to spell out the following words? (REMEMBER that you have to press the numbers in reverse order, so that when you turn the calculator upside down the word will be spelt the right way.)

1. GIGGLE   **2.** SOIL   **3.** GOSH   **4.** HOLE
5. BELLS   **6.** GOBBLE   **7.** BOILS   **8.** BLESSES

The Percent Puzzle***

For the puzzle opposite you will need a paper and pencil as well as your calculator.

Begin at 0 then work out the percentage in the first box and write it down, then work out the next box and subtract that, and so on. If you are right, the answer at the end will be 0.

SOLUTIONS ON PAGE 364.

+ | 0 |

→ | 46% of 2000 | − | 125% of 125 | + | 3% of 4326 | + →

+ | 66.666% of 1000 | + | 96% of 4598 | − | 59% of 5963 | ←

→ | 40% of 4000 | − | 65% of 1000 | − | 1000% of 85 | + →

+ | 2½% of 6542 | − | 16% of 2814 | + | 1% of 4268 | ←

→ | 6% of 6821 | + | 37% of 1895 | + | 116% of 321 | + →

+ | 75% of 6543 | + | 50% of 7500 | − | 55% of 5555 | ←

→ | 25% of 5879 | − | 81% of 8100 | − | 1% of 169767 | = →

| 0 | ←

To the Letter**

To solve these problems you will need to use the following cipher:

A = 1	B = 2	C = 3
D = 4	E = 5	F = 6
G = 7	H = 8	I = 9
J = 10	K = 11	L = 12
M = 13	N = 14	O = 15
P = 16	Q = 17	R = 18
S = 19	T = 20	U = 21
V = 22	W = 23	X = 24
Y = 25	Z = 26	

Using this cipher you can put words into numbers. Using the list of words below, and working letter by letter, with your calculator, multiply the first letter by the second, divide by the third letter, add the fourth and subtract the fifth, and continue multiplying, dividing, adding, and subtracting each letter until you eventually reach the end of the word. Always follow the same order:

$$x \div + -$$

For example, if you were going to do the number code on the word **M O N D A Y**, it would be $13 \times 15 \div 14 + 4 - 1 \times 25$. Use the cipher to 'calculate' the following words.

1. WEDNESDAY
2. FRIDAY
3. SUNDAY
4. JANUARY
5. MARCH
6. APRIL
7. JUNE
8. SEPTEMBER
9. OCTOBER
10. YEAR

Dictionary Digits**

Here are some more calculator words. The answers to the following questions when entered on your calculator, if you turn the display upside down, will look very similar to letters of the alphabet and the answer should spell a whole word.

1. $15^2 - 124 \times 5$ will give you a distress signal.
2. $217 \times 121 - 8,550$ gives you something that goes with a pop.
3. $100,000 - 6,000 + 152 \times 4$ will do something to your mind.

SOLUTIONS ON PAGE 365.

4. The square root of 196 will give you a greeting.

5. .161616 ÷ 4 tells you what Santa Claus said when he fell down the chimney.

6. 44 x 70 will give you a musical instrument.

7. 12,570 + 0.75 x 16 ÷ 333 = an animal.

8. 52,043 ÷ 71 will give you a snakelike fish.

Common Factor*

Calculate the answers to these sums and work out what the calculations have in common.

1. 8 x 473	**2.** 9 x 351
3. 15 x 93	**4.** 21 x 87
5. 27 x 81	**6.** 35 x 41

Multiplication Digits***

The following sums use all the nine digits, 1 to 9, to make up the multiplications and the answers. Work out the digits before checking them on your calculator. In each case you will have to discover what the number is being multiplied by.

1.	1963	**2.**	198	**3.**	1738	**4.**	169
	x ?		x ?		x ?		x ?
	————		———		————		———
	————		———		————		———

The Weigh In**

At a fruit stall on a market, 8 bananas, 7 apples and 3 grapefruit weigh as much as 3 apples, 6 bananas, and 6 grapefruit. If a banana weighs two-thirds as much as a grapefruit and a dozen apples weigh 3 kilograms, how much does a grapefruit weigh?

Add and Subtract**

These four odd-looking equations all have the same things missing – their plus and minus signs. See if you can put them to rights. Each one needs two plus signs and two minus signs arranged correctly in the spaces between the figures in order to make it work out. In the last one, you will also have to move two of the figures together to form one number.

(a) 5 4 3 2 1 = 5
(b) 2 2 3 4 5 = 0
(c) 5 3 1 3 5 = 5
(d) 1 2 3 4 5 6 = 10

999999?*

How could you write the number one hundred with six nines?

Drunkards**

A man can drink a barrel of beer in 20 days, but if his wife also drinks, they can finish the barrel in 14 days. How long would it take the wife to drink the barrel of beer alone?

Keep the Doctor Away*

They do say an apple a day keeps the doctor away, but they also say 'all things in moderation'. This was often said to young Benet, but children have to learn by experience, and the warning of 'Don't eat too many green apples' went unheeded.

So Benet ate two-thirds as many of those green apples as Aaron would have eaten if Aaron had eaten six more than half as many as Benet would have eaten if Benet had eaten three less than Aaron would have eaten.

How many apples does that make the cause of Benet's tummy-ache?

Tea-time*

A cup and saucer together weigh 12 ounces. The cup weighs twice as much as the saucer. How much does the saucer weigh?

Bookworm**

On a shelf is a 6-volume set of books standing side by side in order. Each cover on every volume is 3 millimetres thick, which is 6 millimetres back and front, and text which is 3 centimetres thick. A bookworm has eaten its way straight through the first page of volume 1 through to the last page of volume 6.

How far has the bookworm travelled?

Stick in the Mud*

One-ninth of a log was found stuck in mud, five-sixths was above water, and 2 feet of it was in the water. How long is the log?

Fishy Problem*

A fish's tail weighs nine pounds. Its head weighs as much as the tail and one-third of the body combined, and the body weighs as much as the head and tail combined. What does the whole fish weigh?

SOLUTIONS ON PAGES 365 AND 366.

Number Scrabble***

Each of the letters below corresponds uniquely to a numerical digit. Find the correspondence to make this digit correct.

```
    A  L  P  H  A  B  E  T

 +  L  E  T  T  E  R  S
    _____

    S  C  R  A  B  B  L  E
    _____
```

Baby Monkeys*

If a baby monkey weighs three-quarters of a baby monkey plus three quarters of a pound, how much does a baby monkey weigh?

Farm Fare*

A farmer, being asked what number of animals he kept on his farm, answered, 'They're all horses but two, all sheep but two, and all pigs but two.'
How many animals did he have in all?

Talking Turkey*

If a turkey weighs 10 kg and a half of its own weight, what does the turkey weigh?

What's the Difference?**

What is the difference between 4 square kilometres and 4 kilometres square?

Two Dozen**

Using just three digits, write out a simple addition sum that totals 24. The digits must all be the same, but they can't be 8!

Four Fives*

Use four fives to make 6½!

SOLUTIONS ON PAGE 366.

Sum Subtraction!***

Take 45 away from 45 and leave 45 as the remainder! If you think it can't be done, think again. Here's one way:

$$
\begin{array}{r}
987654321 = 45 \\
-123456789 = 45 \\
\hline
864197532 = 45 \\
\hline
\end{array}
$$

Using the same system, can you find another way?

Ten Not Out*

Look at this carefully:

Now make TEN out of it by adding only five more lines.

Father and Son**

A son asked his father how old he was and this is the reply his father gave him: 'Your age is now one quarter of mine, but five years ago it was only one-fifth.' How old is the father?

Fowl-up**

Let's end with a really fowl problem! If a hen and a half lays an egg and a half in a day and a half, how many eggs will 6 hens lay in 7 days?

SOLUTIONS ON PAGE 366.

PICTURE PUZZLES

SECTION TWO

Spot the Difference 3. Departure Time

A and B are almost identical pictures but picture B has fourteen differences. Can you spot them?

SOLUTION ON PAGE 360.

Maze 4**

Spot the Mistake 3. Ex Libris**

What's wrong in this library?

SOLUTION ON PAGE 360.

Maze 5**

Maze 6**

Maze 7**

Maze 8**

Shadow Shows**

In Victorian times shadow shows were a popular form of home entertainment. With the use of a lamp projected on a blank wall, and a skilled pair of hands, the shadows of a variety of people and creatures could be created. Here are some of the hand positions for casting interesting shadows. Can you say what the shadow would be in each case?

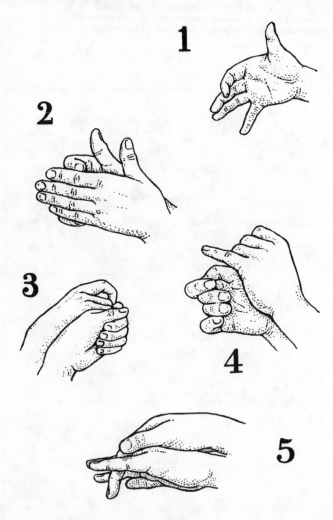

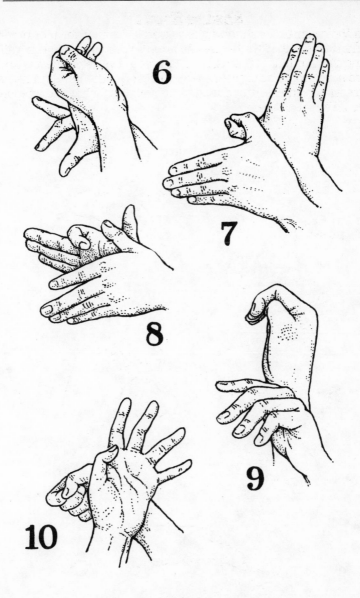

6

7

8

9

10

SOLUTIONS ON PAGE 360.

BRAINTEASERS
AND
MIND ENDERS

Value the Difference*

Is there any difference in value between six dozen dozen and a half dozen dozen?

Family Problems**

A boy has as many sisters as he has brothers, but each of his sisters has twice as many brothers as she has sisters. How many boys and girls are there in the family?

Poor but Honest*

How many of these riddles can you answer?

1. Why must a dishonest man stay indoors?
2. Why is an honest friend like orange chips?
3. What men are above board in their movements?
4. Why is a false friend like your shadow?
5. What kind of vice is it that people dislike if they are ever so bad?
6. Who is the oldest lunatic on record?
7. Why did the moron throw all his nails away?
8. What is the height of folly?
9. Why is a blockhead deserving of promotion?
10. What are the most unsociable things in the world?
11. What is more to be admired than a promising young man?
12. What chasm often separates friends?
13. Where lies the path of duty?
14. What is the best way to keep loafers from standing on the street corner?
15. Why should you always remain calm when you encounter cannibals?

Brief Encounter*

Lady Constance met the Countess of Kensington in the laun-

derette. 'Don't I know you?' enquired Lady Constance.
'You certainly ought to,' replied the Countess.
'Your mother was my mother's only daughter.'
How are they related?

Four of a Kind**

It's no laughing matter to have to find a common English word of
eight letters which contains four Gs. Try.

Poetical Problem***

Curtail me thrice, I am a youth;
Behead me once, a snake;
Complete, I'm often used, in truth,
When upward steps you take.

Who or what am I?

Easy**

The beginning of eternity,
The end of time and space,
The beginning of every end,
The end of every place.

What can be described in this way?

Which Way?***

You find yourself in the strange country of Everywhere and have
lost your way. You could be in the town of Here or There. All the
inhabitants of Here tell the truth, but the inhabitants of There
always tell lies. As you walk down the street you see a man
approaching and you know that he is either from Here or There.
What one question would you ask him to find out where you are?

Choral Conundrum?*

Add the bottom of a woman's dress to an insect and you will get a
musical number sung by a church choir.

What is the word?

SOLUTIONS ON PAGE 367.

Cat-astrophe*

If three cunning cats can catch three masterful mice in three minutes, how many cunning cats could catch one hundred masterful mice in one hundred minutes?

Russian Riddle*
Solve the following puzzle in under 30 seconds.

Two Russians walk down a street in Moscow. One Russian is the father of the other Russian's son. How are they related?

Jumbled Letters*

Unscramble the following letters so that they spell just one word:

NETOUSDJORW

Aunts and Uncles**

A man and his sister were out walking together one Saturday morning. The man pointed across the street to a boy and said: 'That boy is my nephew.' The woman replied: 'He is not *my* nephew.' Can you explain this?

The Whole Lot*

How much dirt is there in a hole 3 metres deep and 1 metre square?

Revolutionary Conundrum*

Add a girl's name from a famous American battle to an ancient Roman garment, and what do you get?

False or True*

Some of these statements are true. Some are false. Can you spot the false ones?

1. Until 1957 it was illegal to go swimming in the State of New York on a Sunday.

2. Teddy bears were named after the American President Theodore Roosevelt.

SOLUTIONS ON PAGE 367.

3. In southern Italy tulips are not only grown because they are nice to look at, but also because they are considered a delicacy and are regularly eaten as part of a salad.

4. Typewriters were first developed to help the blind.

5. Benjamin Franklin invented the digital clock in 1777.

6. An earthworm can pull ten times its own weight.

7. Originally the yo-yo was a Filipino jungle weapon.

8. Cars were first started by ignition keys in 1949.

9. William Lee invented a knitting machine in 1589.

10. Indian ink actually comes from China.

11. The oldest account of a chimney describes one in Venice in 1347.

12. President Dwight Eisenhower was once North American Monopoly Champion.

13. Cleopatra was the product of six generations of brother/sister marriages.

14. Elephants cannot jump.

15. No mammal has poisonous glands.

16. A gorilla's brain weighs 10 lb.

17. The Romans used weasels to catch mice.

18. Only male nightingales sing.

19. The Emperor Napoleon was an alcoholic.

20. Ovid wrote a book about cosmetics.

21. It is recorded that Louis XIII of France was bled forty-seven times in one month.

22. Queen Marie Antoinette of France and the actress Jayne Mansfield had identical bust measurements.

23. 'School' is derived from the Greek word Skhole which means 'leisure'.

24. Six different dialects are spoken in India.

25. During their studies medical students increase their vocabulary by 10,000 words.

SOLUTIONS ON PAGES 367 AND 368.

Three Dimensional Shapes**

Here are some patterns for solid forms. Which pattern would make up which figure?

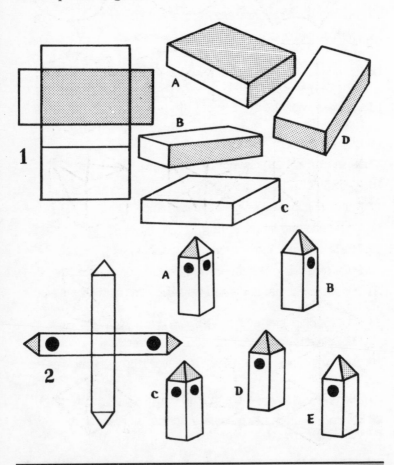

SOLUTIONS ON PAGE 368.

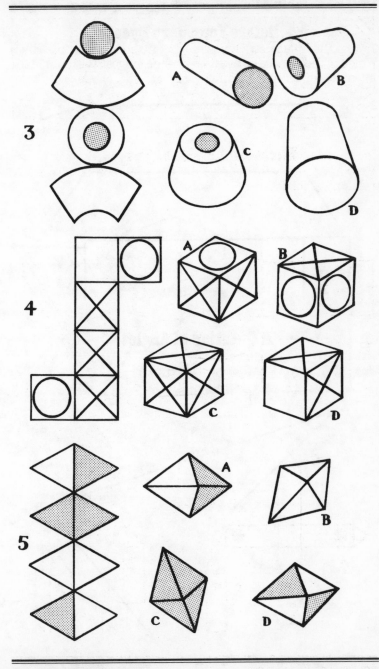

3

4

5

Before Your Very Eyes*

Try out these geometric puzzlers: but no cheating with a ruler!
Which of these three straight lines is the longest: the top one, the
middle one or the bottom one?

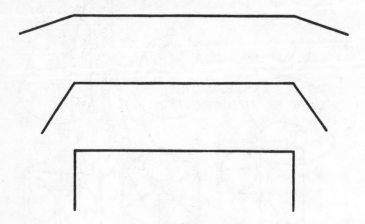

A Question of Angles*

Which is the longest line:
The one from A to C or the one from B to D?

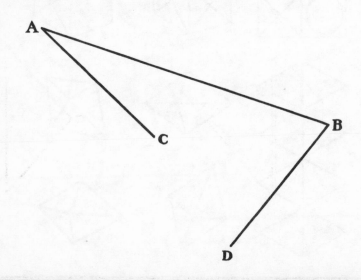

The Distance*

Is B nearer to A
or nearer to C.

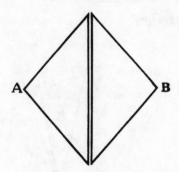

SOLUTION ON PAGE 368.

A Matter of Size**

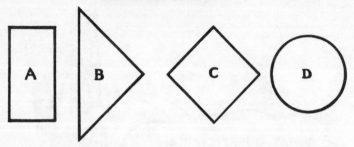

Above are 4 fields. Which is the largest and which the smallest?

Curious Cube**

From which angle are we looking at this cube? Is it viewed from above or from below? Is the line across the corner of the cube straight or bent?

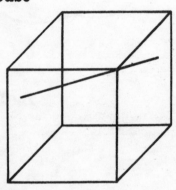

Right Angles*

Which is the largest angle: Angle A or angle B?

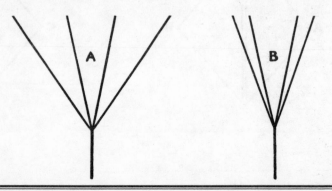

Key to the Problem**

Here are six bunches of keys. On each key ring only TWO keys are identical, the rest are different. Can you say which is a pair in each case?

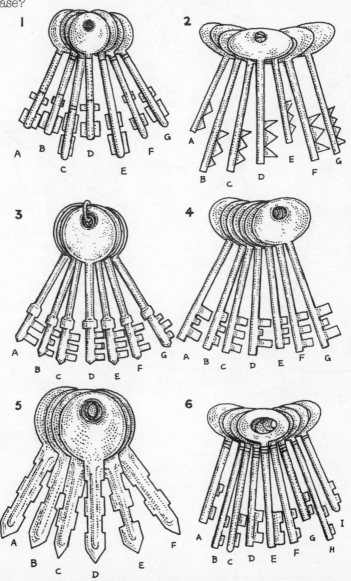

SOLUTIONS ON PAGE 368.

Triangular Terror*

How many triangles are there in the figure below?

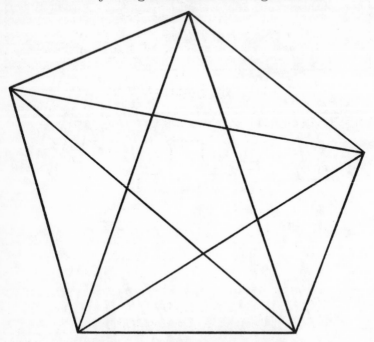

Mystery of the Sphinx***

Can you solve the mystery of the Sphinx? All you have to do is divide the figure into 4 equal parts, each one being a miniature of the Sphinx shape but they can be placed upside down or sideways. It is possible!

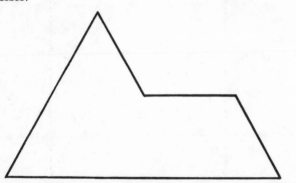

All Square*

Cut this figure into 4 pieces, each of the same size and shape, that will fit together and form a perfect square.

Square and Triangle**

Take a square piece of paper and fold it so as to form the largest possible equilateral triangle. The triangle in which the sides are the same length as those of the square, as shown in the diagram, will *not* be the largest possible. No markings or measurements may be made except by the creases themselves.

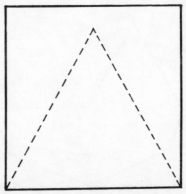

SOLUTIONS ON PAGES 368 AND 369.

Paper Letter**

Cut out the shapes below from a piece of paper or card. Put them together to form a certain letter of the alphabet. Which letter is it?

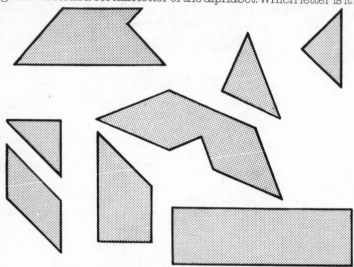

Folding an Octagon**

Can you cut a regular octagon from a square piece of paper without using compasses or ruler or anything but scissors? You can fold the paper so as to make creases.

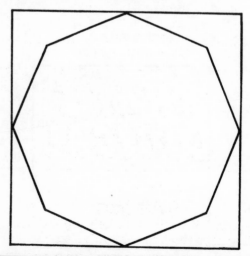

Biggest Hole in the World***

This puzzle sounds impossible, but it isn't! All you need is a sheet of ordinary writing paper and a pair of scissors. What you have to do is cut a hole in the paper large enough for you to climb through! When you have completed the puzzle you should have a hole large enough for you to place the paper over your head, pass it over your body, and step through it without tearing it. It can be done, honestly!

Pinhole Puzzle*

Take two pieces of card. A visiting card or playing card will do. In one of the cards prick three very small holes with the point of a pin. These must be very close together so that they do not cover an area greater than the pupil of the eye. In the second piece of card prick one single pin hole. Now, hold the card with the three pinholes as close to your eye as possible, and the other card with one pinhole about 2 or 3 inches (5 cm) away from the first. On looking through the first card, what appears to happen to the second?

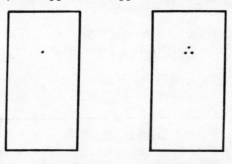

Quick Quiz*

1. Folk is spelt F.O.L.K. *not* F.O.K.E. Joke is spelt J.O.K.E. *not* J.O.L.K. How do you spell the white of an egg?

SOLUTIONS ON PAGE 369.

2. How many grooves are there on a gramophone record that revolves at 45 r.p.m.? And how many are there on one that revolves at 33⅓ r.p.m.?

3. Mr Broke the Banker has two coins in his left-hand pocket. Together they add up to 60p. One of them is not a 50p piece, so what are the two coins?

4. What do you find right in the middle of Glasgow?

5. What one word in the Oxford English Dictionary do people from Chicago always pronounce incorrectly?

6. In a leap year, how many months have 28 days?

7. What do you get if you add 2 to 200 four times?

8. If I have 467 large conkers and 193 small conkers in my prize conker collection and I take away all but a dozen of them, how many will I have left?

9. In the whole history of the world, have New Year's Eve and New Year's Day ever fallen in the same year?

10. I own something round and flat and black and shiny with a small hole right in the middle of it. Is this a record?

One Number*

If you add 1,000 to a certain whole number, the result will be actually more than if you multiplied that number by 1,000! What's the number?

Unlucky Thirteen*

Here are thirteen letters:

J F M A M R J J A S O N D

One of them doesn't belong to the series. Which one?

SOLUTIONS ON PAGE 370.

Lewis Carroll's Puzzles**

The creator of Alice in Wonderland and Through the Looking Glass was also an enthusiastic puzzler. Here are five of his favourite brainteasers.

1. John gave his brother James a box:
   About it there were many locks.
   James woke and said it gave him pain;
   So gave it back to John again.
   The box was not with lid supplied
   Yet caused two lids to open wide:
   And all these locks had never a key
   What kind of box, then, could it be?

2. Three sisters at breakfast were feeding the cat.
   The first gave it sole, Puss was grateful for that:
   The next gave it salmon, which Puss thought a treat:
   The third gave it herring, which Puss wouldn't eat.

   Explain the conduct of the cat.

3. When the King found that his money was nearly all gone, and that he really must live more economically, he decided on sending away most of his Wise Men. There were some hundreds of them, all very fine old men, and magnificently dressed in green velvet gowns with gold buttons. If they had a fault, it was that they always contradicted one another when he asked for their advice, and they certainly ate and drank enormously. So, on the whole, he was rather glad to get rid of them. But there was an old law, which he did not dare to disobey, which said that there must always be:

   Seven blind of both eyes:
   Ten blind of one eye:
   Five that see with both eyes:
   Nine that see with one eye.

   Query: How many did he keep?

4. Below are three pairs of statements. What conclusion can you draw from each of the pairs? For example, if you were told 'No professors are ignorant' and 'All ignorant people are vain', the

conclusion you would draw would be that 'No professors are vain.' Now try these.

   1. No doctors are enthusiastic.
      You are enthusiastic.

   2. Dictionaries are useful.
      Useful books are valuable.

   3. No misers are unselfish.
      None but misers save bottle tops.

5. If seventy percent of people in an old folks home have lost an eye, seventy-five percent have lost an ear, eighty percent have lost an arm, and eighty-five percent a leg – what percentage at least must have lost all four?

The Bridge Problem***

Four ladies – Avril, Betty, Connie and Davina – and three men – Ernest, Frank, and George – all play bridge together. It is a card game for four players.

1. One evening they played four bridge games in which the partners were:
   Avril and Ernest versus Betty and Frank
   Avril and George versus Davina and Frank
   Betty and Connie versus Frank and George
   Connie and Ernest versus Davina and George

2. No more than one married couple ever play in the same game.

3. The members of each married couple are never partners in a game.

4. The men and women consist of three married couples and a widow.

Who is the widow?

Death by Drowning***

Anthony, Bob and Charles were questioned by a detective about Dolly's death by drowning.

1. Anthony said: If it was murder, Bob did it.

SOLUTIONS ON PAGE 370.

2. Bob said: If it was murder, I did not do it.

3. Charles said: If it was not murder, it was suicide.

4. The detective said truthfully: If just one of these three men lied it was suicide.

How did Dolly die? Was it accident, suicide or murder?

Marriage Lines**

Messrs Lagan, Foyle, Bann and Erne are neighbours. Three of them are married. One of the four is bald, one redheaded and one dark-haired.

Mr Erne isn't redheaded, nor is he dark-haired, but is married.
Mr Lagan isn't bald nor is he fairhaired, but is single.
Mrs Bann is blonde but her husband is neither dark-haired nor bald.
Mr Foyle doesn't have either fair or dark hair.
Mr Erne's wife is dark-haired while the bald-headed man has a redheaded wife.

With this set of facts, can you work out the following:

1. Whose wife is a redhead?
2. What colour hair has the single man?
3. Mrs Foyle's husband has which hair colour?

Mad Cap***

The King of Sellonica needed a man of great courage and wisdom for a very important mission. Unable to decide which of his three best knights should do the job, he called them to him and had them blindfolded. Then he placed a cap on the head of each one and said:

'Each of you now wears either a black or a white cap. When the blindfolds are removed, I want you to raise your hand as soon as you see a black cap. Drop your hand as soon as you know the colour of your own cap.'

The blindfolds were removed, and all the knights raised their hands immediately, for the wily old man had placed a black cap on each knight's head. After a few minutes one courtier dropped his hand and said:

'My cap is black.'

By what logical reasoning had he reached that conclusion?

A Hit or a Miss**

The teacher asked Billy a question:

'If a certain missile will hit its target one out of four times, and four such missiles are fired at one target, then what is the probability that the target will be hit?'

'That's simple,' replied Billy, 'it's a certainty one missile will hit the target.' Was he right?

One Word*

There is one everyday English word which, when printed in capital letters, reads exactly the same upside down as it does the right way up. What's the word?

A Time Teaser**

When you see the reflection of a clock in a mirror and the time appears to be 2.30, what time is it really?

Letters Salad*

Here are five rows of letters:

```
I  C  A  C
I  C  A  B
I  C  A  J
I  C  A  U
I  C  A  Z
```

One of the rows doesn't belong to the series. Which one?

What's Hot*

It burns no coal, no oil, no gas and it has no need of electricity, and yet it is far hotter than all the ovens and fires and blast furnaces in the United States when they are heated to capacity. What is it?

SOLUTIONS ON PAGE 371.

Alarming*

If on the last day of February 1980 – and remember, 1980 was a leap year – you had gone to bed at seven o'clock, having set your alarm clock to wake you up at 8.15 a.m. how much sleep would you have got?

Twin Twister*

Jack and Jill were born on the same day in the same year and are the children of the same parents – and yet they are not twins. How come?

Train Trial*

A boy is on a train, which is travelling at 60 miles per hour. He jumps straight up in the air 3 feet. Where does he land?

WHAT SHIP HAS TWO MATES BUT NO CAPTAIN?

COURTSHIP.

SOLUTIONS ON PAGE 371.

Charades**

Here is a Victorian charade puzzle. Like the game of charades, the versified clues provide the separate syllables of a word, and then finally the complete word. Your task is to identify the mystery word.

> In the early spring, one silent night,
> The bold Sir Wilfred strayed
> Beneath his lady's lattice bright,
> To sing a serenade.
> He sat him down upon my *first*
> And there his loving lay rehearsed.
>
> A silvery mist hung o'er the scene
> Where thus he breathed his vows;
> And dewdrops gemmed the herbage green,
> And decked the budding boughs.
> But ah! Sir Wilfred should have reckoned
> The grass was sure to be my *second*.
>
> Next morn he did his foot page call,
> And bade at once repair
> To gay Lord Guthlac's festival hall,
> And him this message bear:
> 'Tell hib I'b ill, upod by soul!
> And can't todight attend by *whole*!'

Letter by Letter***

Here are 9 words which have something important in common. What is it?

1. Brandy
2. Chastens
3. Craters
4. Grangers
5. Pirated
6. Scampi
7. Stores
8. Swingers
9. Tramps

That's Cricket**

Two bowlers during the season have each taken 28 wickets for 60 runs. One bowler in the next match takes 4 wickets for 36 runs, and the other takes 1 wicket for 27 runs.

Which now has the best average?

SOLUTIONS ON PAGE 371.

Plural Puzzle***
Can you supply the plural for each of these words?

1. Daughter-in-law
2. Attorney general
3. Brigadier general
4. Judge advocate
5. Chargé d'affaires
6. Potato
7. Notary public
8. Law merchant
9. Opus
10. Pelvis
11. Sergeant major
12. Teaspoonful
13. Piccolo
14. Table d'hôte
15. Court martial
16. Paymaster general
17. Mister
18. Madam
19. Crisis
20. Man of war
21. Lieutenant colonel
22. Bandit
23. Cannon
24. Phenomenon
25. Aviatrix
26. Manservant
27. Oboe
28. Ox
29. Valet de chambre
30. Datum

SOLUTIONS ON PAGES 371 AND 372.

Special Feature***

Here is a limerick with a very special feature. What is it?

When an expert burlesque queen named Maizy,
Stripping velvet, became very lazy.
She would quickly exhibit
Just one jewelled explicit,
Gliding off from the jokesters like crazy.

Underground Stations*

Each of a dozen well known London Underground Stations has had part of its name removed and the missing part replaced by a clue to it in brackets. How many of the dozen can you identify?

1. (compass point) minster
2. Le(frozen water)ster Square
3. E(you and me)ton
4. (conqueror) ia
5. B(be without) friars
6. (Draw along)er Hill
7. C(running very fast) Cross
8. (cook by dry heat) r Street
9. King(lean unsteadily)
10. (inexperienced) Park
11. (leave in difficulties or run aground)
12. (big animal) and (fortress)

Beauty Queens***

Of the three finalists in the bathing beauty contest, Amelia is older than the redhead, but younger than the hairdresser. Bernice is younger than the blonde, whilst Caroline is older than the brunette. The typist is the receptionist's younger sister. Can you give the hair colouring and profession of each girl in order of age?

Find the Number**

Find a four digit number which satisfies each of the three following conditions:
1. The last digit is twice the first digit.
2. The third digit is twice the second digit.
3. The sum of the first and last digits is twice the third digit.

SOLUTIONS ON PAGE 372.

All in the Family**

A man has three sons, and each of his sons has three sons. Using this information, answer the following questions.

> 1. How many pairs of cousins are there?
> 2. How many pairs of father and son?
> 3. How many pairs of brothers?
> 4. How many pairs of uncle and nephew?
> 5. How many pairs of grandfather and grandson?
> 6. How many people are there in the group?

Remember that one man may be in any number of pairs. He and his father are one pair, the same man and his son are another pair.

Liquid Refreshment*

If you were given a 5-pint container and a 3-pint container, how could you measure out 1 pint of liquid?

You have an unlimited supply of liquid with which to do this puzzle.

SOLUTIONS ON PAGE 372.

PICTURE PUZZLES
SECTION THREE

Spot the Difference 4. School's Out***

Can you spot twelve distinct differences on picture B compared with picture A?

Spot the Mistake 4. Victorian Parlour***

Here is a typical parlour the day after Prince Albert's death except that some things are out of place. Which are they?

SOLUTIONS ON PAGE 361.

Maze 9***

Maze 10***

Spot the Mistake 5. Pharaoh's Folly***

This artist's impression of Pharaoh's tomb is a little too free. Can you spot the inaccuracies?

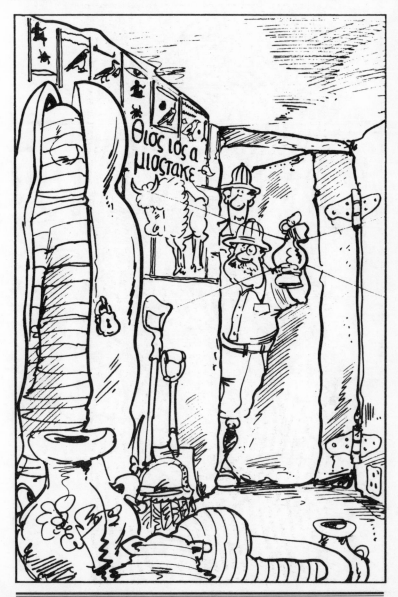

Spot the Difference 5. Waiter***

Can you spot twelve distinct differences on picture B compared with picture A?

B

SOLUTION ON PAGE 361.

See if you can strike it lucky by solving all these unmatchable puzzles, for which you will need nothing more than a box of matches.

Triangular Trouble*

1. Take 9 matches and lay them out in 3 triangles:

Now see if you can make 5 triangles by moving just 3 of the matches.

2. Lay down six matches to make this pattern:

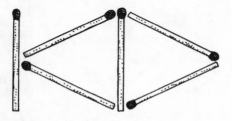

Move 3 of these matches to make 6 equilateral triangles.

3. With 5 matches see if you can make 2 triangles.

4. Take 9 matches and with them make 5 triangles.

SOLUTIONS ON PAGE 373.

5. Take sixteen matches and make up this pattern:

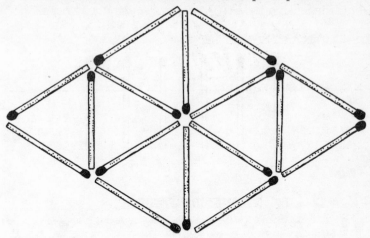

Remove 4 matches and leave just 4 triangles.

Matcho**

Remove four of the matches in this pattern and leave nine squares:

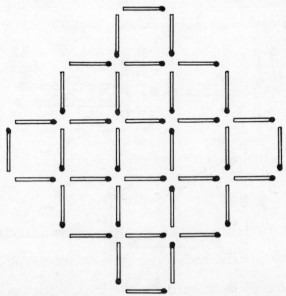

SOLUTIONS ON PAGE 373.

MatheMATCHics*

Here are some matheMATCHical puzzles using matchsticks:

1. Set out six matches like this:

Now add 5 more to make 9.

2. Move just 1 match to make this Roman sum work:

3. Make this sum correct by adding just 1 match:

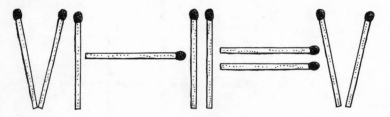

4. Move 2 matches to make this sum correct:

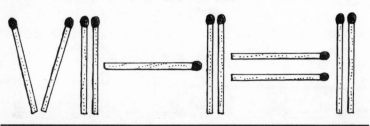

SOLUTIONS ON PAGE 373.

5. Remove 3 matches to make this sum correct:

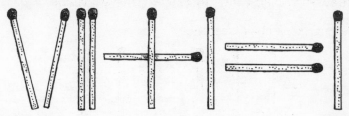

6. This sum will be right if you move just 1 match:

7. Make this sum correct without moving any matches:

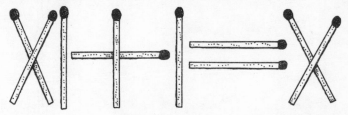

Untouchables***

This puzzle will really set you thinking. Take six matches and arrange them on the table in such a way that each match is touching the other five. It can be done!

All You Need*

With 16 matches create 4 squares like this:

SOLUTIONS ON PAGES 373 AND 374.

Now take away 4 of the matches, move 3 of the remaining ones and see if you can end up with what it is that makes the world go round.

Long Division**
With 16 matches form a figure like this:

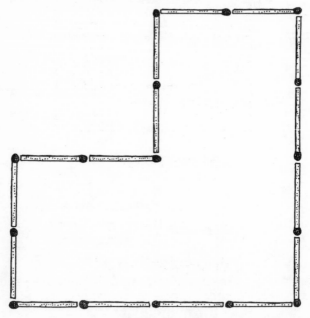

Now add 8 more matches and divide the shape into 4 equal parts.

First Square*
This puzzle should not cause you too much trouble. Take the 6 lowest dominoes in the set, the 0/0, the 0/1, the 0/2, the 1/1, the 1/2

SOLUTIONS ON PAGE 374.

and the 2/2, and arrange them in a square so that all the joins match in number. The shape of the square should be just like this one:

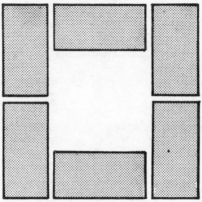

Second Square**

Take the same six dominoes as you used in the First Square, the 0/0, the 0/1, the 0/2, the 1/1, the 1/2 and the 2/2, and arrange them in exactly the same shape, but this time do it so that each of the four sides of the square contains the same number of pips.

Triangular Terror**

For this puzzle you require the same 6 dominoes as above. Arrange them to form an equilateral triangle like the one below.

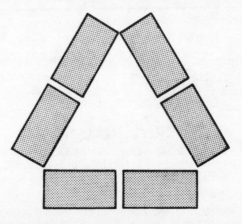

SOLUTIONS ON PAGE 374.

The problem is that you must make sure that each of the three sides of the triangle contains exactly the same number of pips, but at the same time you must make sure that none of the joins match.

First Rectangle**

Since we've had a couple of square problems and a triangular one, it's about time we had a rectangular one. For this you'll need the same 6 dominoes, the 0/0, the 0/1, the 0/2, the 1/1, the 1/2, the 2/2, and the same quick wittedness as before. You have got to use the dominoes to create a rectangle that looks exactly like this:

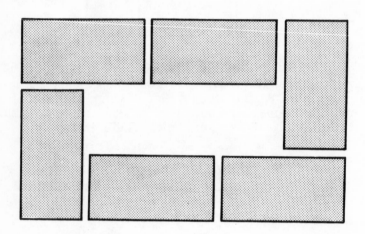

The puzzling part of the problem comes in making sure that each of the four sides of the rectangle contains precisely the same number of pips.

The Three Rectangles**

Take the fifteen lowest dominoes in the set (the 0/0, the 0/1, the 0/2, the 0/3, the 0/4, the 1/1, the 1/2, the 1/3, the 1/4, the 2/2, the 2/3, the 2/4, the 3/3, the 3/4, the 4/4) and form 3 separate rectangles with them, so that all the joins are matching. Each of the rectangles should look like the one at the top of page 323

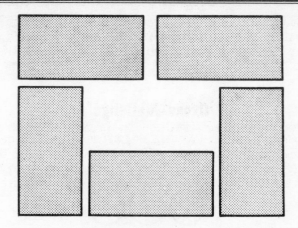

Giant Square***

Take the 10 lowest dominoes in the set (the 0/0, the 0/1, the 0/2, the 0/3, the 1/1, the 1/2, the 1/3, the 2/2, the 2/3 and the 3/3) but you must make sure that the number of pips on each of the 4 sides of the Giant Square is the same and that none of the joins match. Here's the shape you should create for this puzzle:

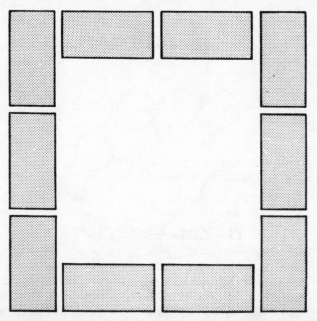

SOLUTION ON PAGE 375.

COIN PUZZLES

Cross Challenge*

Take six coins and arrange them on the table in the shape of a cross, like this:

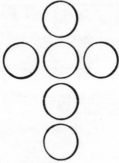

Now move just one of the coins and create two rows with four coins in each row.

Square Challenge*

Take 12 coins and arrange them on the table in the shape of a square, like this:

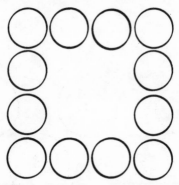

As you can see, there are four coins along each side of the square. Using the same 12 coins, form another square, but with the new square, see to it that you can count five coins along each side.

SOLUTIONS ON PAGE 375.

Circular Challenge**

Take 6 coins and lay them out on the table in two columns like this:

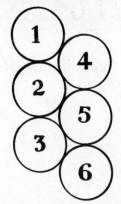

Now all you've got to do is make a circle of coins in just three moves! You can only move one coin at a time and once you've moved it to its new position it must be touching at least two other coins.

Pyramid Challenge**

Take 10 coins and lay them out on the table in the shape of a pyramid, like this:

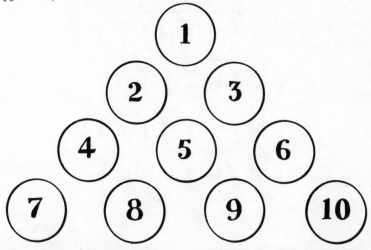

Now move just three of the coins and turn the pyramid upside down.

SOLUTIONS ON PAGE 376.

The H Problem**

Take seven coins and arrange them in a pattern to look like the letter H.

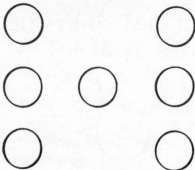

As you can see, counting the diagonal lines as well as the vertical and horizontal, you have five rows with three coins in each row. Now add an extra two coins to the pattern and create a new pattern that incorporates ten rows with three coins in each row.

Sixteen Coins**

Take sixteen coins and arrange them on the table in four columns, with heads and tails alternating, like this:

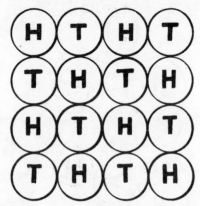

Now all you've got to do is rearrange the coins so that the coins in each of the four vertical columns are alike. That's to say you've got to end up with one column of heads, one column of tails, one of heads, one of tails. The only problem is: your hand is only allowed to touch *two* of the sixteen coins!

SOLUTIONS ON PAGE 376.

Six in a Row**

Find three 5p pieces and three 10p pieces and lay them out in a neat row, like this:

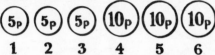

Now, in just three moves, moving two adjacent coins at a time, you have got to make a row of coins where the 10p and the 5p pieces *alternate*. There must be no gaps between the coins.

Eight in a Row**

Find four 5p pieces and four 10p pieces and lay them out in a row, like this:

Now, in four moves, moving two adjacent coins at a time, you have got to make a row in which there are no gaps and the 10p and 5p pieces alternate.

Head Over Heels***

Take eight coins and lay them out in a circle, all heads up and looking like this:

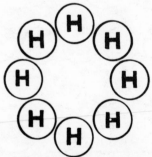

Starting from any coin you like, and moving clockwise, or anti-clockwise, count one, two, three, four, and turn over the fourth coin so that it's tails up. Starting again from any coin that's heads up, repeat the process. Keep at it until all the coins but one are tails up.

SOLUTIONS ON PAGES 376 AND 377.

Nine-a-side**

Take thirty-two coins and lay them out in a square so that there are nine coins on each side of the square.

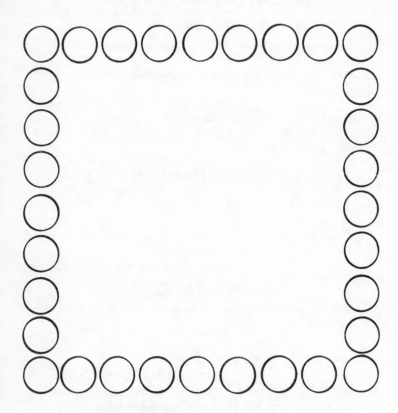

Now remove four coins and rearrange the remaining twenty-eight so that there are still nine coins on each side of the square.

Now remove a further four coins and rearrange the remaining twenty-four so that there are still nine coins on each side of the square!

Finally, remove four more coins and rearrange the twenty that are left so that you can still count nine coins on each side of the square!

SOLUTION ON PAGE 377.

Odd Lines*

Take twelve coins and lay them out in a very familiar pattern, so that you end up with three straight lines and an odd number of coins in each line.

Seven Rows*

Take twelve coins and lay them out in seven rows, with four coins in each row.

Nine Rows**

Take nineteen coins and lay them out in nine rows, with five coins in each row.

Twelve Rows***

Take twenty-one coins and lay them out in twelve rows with five coins in each row.

Fifteen Rows***

Take sixteen coins and lay them out in fifteen rows, with four coins in each row.

WHY ARE CONUNDRUMS THAT CANNOT BE SOLVED LIKE A MAN DISAPPOINTED BY HIS VISITORS?

BECAUSE THERE IS A HOST PUT OUT AND NOT ONE GUESSED.

SOLUTIONS ON PAGES 377 AND 378.

TANGRAMS

A tangram is a geometric dissection puzzle, devised in ancient China, in which seven standard pieces (two small triangles, one medium size triangle, two large triangles, one square and one rhomboid) are used to make images of various objects. To attempt these puzzles you will need a set of tangrams, which can be cut from a single square like this:

Shapely Tangrams*

Use all your tangrams to create each of these shapes.

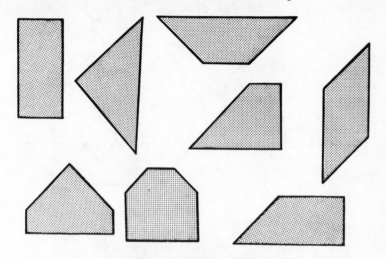

Number Tangrams**

With your tangrams try to construct, one at a time, the numbers one, two, three, four, five, six, seven, and eight, as shown.

SOLUTIONS ON PAGES 378 AND 379.

Alphabetical Tangrams***

Attempt to construct the entire alphabet with your tangrams, one letter at a time. You must use all seven pieces and none of them must overlap.

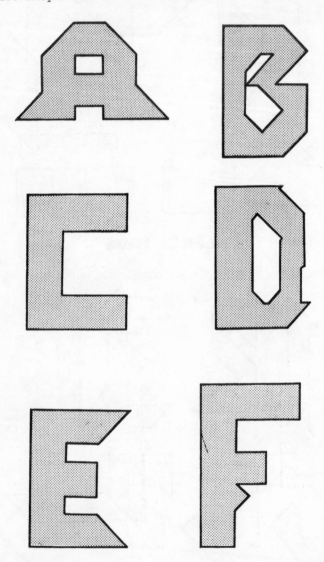

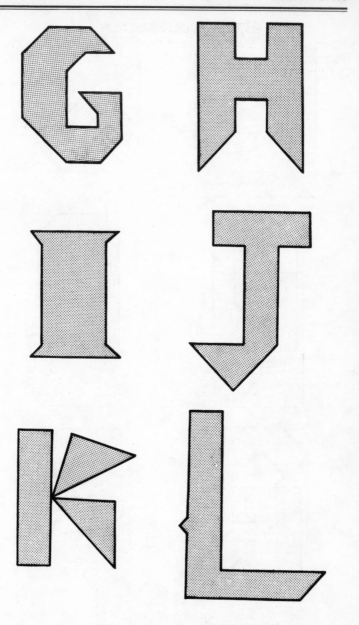

SOLUTIONS ON PAGES 379 AND 380.

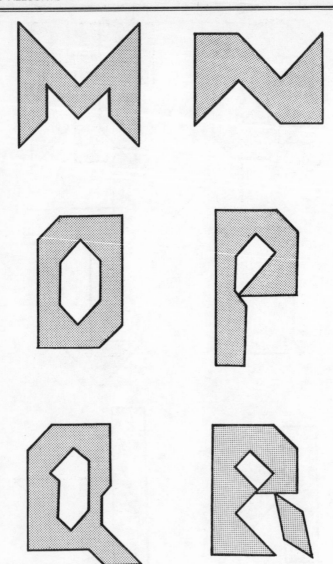

SOLUTIONS ON PAGE 380.

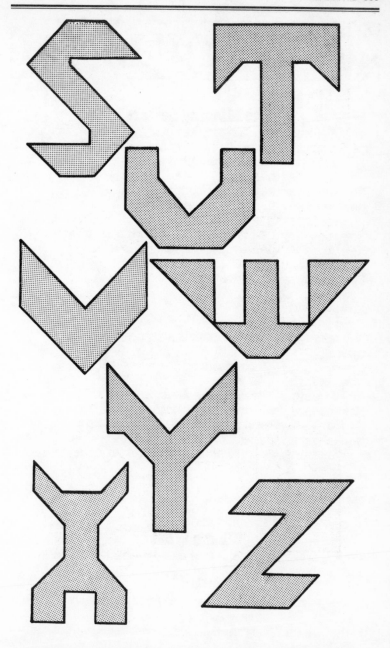

MIXED BAG

The Missing Letters*

Here is a puzzle that's easy to work out if you do it with pencil and paper, but pretty perplexing if you try it without – so try it without.

Think of all the letters of the alphabet.

Now take away the second.

Now take away the twenty-second.

Now take away the one that comes before the last one you took away.

Now take away the letter O and the letter that comes after O.

Now take away the sixth, fifth and fourth letters.

Now take away X and Y.

Now take away the third letter.

Now add Q.

Now take away T.

Now take away the seventh letter.

Now take away H and the letter that comes seven places before it.

Now take away the letter that comes before R.

Now take away R.

Now take away the remaining vowel.

Now take away the three letters that follow it.

Now take away N and the letter that comes before it.

Now take away the last letter of the alphabet.

Now take away all the remaining consonants in the word 'stew'.

What are you left with?

What's What*

Here are twenty questions to make you think. They aren't as simple as they sound.

1. What is it that no one wishes to have, but no one wishes to lose?
2. What is it that everyone believes is always coming, but never really arrives?

3. What is it that you can't hold for half an hour, even though it's lighter than feather?
4. What is it that's put on the table, cut and passed, but never eaten?
5. What is it that occurs four times in every week, twice in every month, but only once in a year?
6. What is full of holes, but still holds water?
7. What is the one thing you break when you name it?
8. What is always in front of you, even though you can never see it?
9. What is lengthened by being cut at both ends?
10. What always weighs the same, whatever its size?
11. What is large enough to hold a pig and yet small enough to hold in your hand?
12. What is it that the person who makes it doesn't need, the person who buys it doesn't use for himself and the person who uses it does so without knowing it?
13. What is it that everyone, no matter how careful they happen to be, always overlooks?
14. What can be right, but never wrong?
15. What lives on its own substance, but dies the moment it has devoured itself?
16. What is it that has no length, no breadth, no thickness, but when it is given to you you definitely feel?
17. What is bought by the yard, but worn out by the foot?
18. What will always be down however high up it is?
19. What goes from New York to Philadelphia without moving?
20. With what could you fill a barrel to make it lighter than when it is empty?

My Three Sons*

I have a Russian friend who has three sons. The first son was called Rab and became a lawyer. The second son was called Ymra and became a soldier. The third son became a sailor.

What was he called?
Why?

Oddition*

Write down five odd numbers so that when you add them up they total 14.

SOLUTIONS ON PAGE 381.

Musical Meanings*

Here are some well-known musical terms. All you've got to do is work out their meanings.

1. Does **presto** mean:
   a) fast?
   b) slow?
   c) quietly?
   d) loudly?

2. Does **adagio** mean:
   a) very lightly?
   b) very quickly?
   c) very bouncily?
   d) very slowly?

3. Does **largo** mean:
   a) in the style of a lively dance?
   b) in the style of a funeral march?
   c) in a fast, raucous style?
   d) in a slow, dignified style?

4. Does **fortissimo** mean:
   a) very fast?
   b) very slow?
   c) very loud?
   d) very soft?

5. Does **dolce** mean:
   a) angrily?
   b) sorrowfully?
   c) sweetly?
   d) tearfully?

6. Does **crescendo** mean:
   a) singing very loudly?
   b) decreasing the volume slowly?
   c) singing very softly?
   d) increasing the volume slowly?

Weak Word**

Can you think of a fifteen-letter word in which the only vowel is the letter E which is used three times in the word?

Unpunctuated*

All punctuation has been omitted in the strange sentences that follow. Can you supply the correct punctuation and make sense of them? To make it more complicated, they are not necessarily single sentences.

1. he said that that that that woman said ought to have been which

2. it was and I said not but

3. the murderer spoke angrily half an hour after he was hanged

4. time flies you cannot they pass by at such irregular intervals

SOLUTIONS ON PAGE 381.

5. Esau Wood saw a saw saw wood as no other wood saw Wood saw would saw wood of all the wood saws Wood ever saw saw wood Wood never saw a wood saw that would saw wood as the wood saw Wood saw saw wood would saw wood and I never saw a wood saw that would saw wood as the wood saw Wood saw would saw until I saw Wood saw wood with the wood saw Esau Wood saw saw wood.

When you've punctuated number five try saying it to yourself ten times without making any mistakes!

Composers' Corner*

Here, listed in the order of their birth, are the names of some of the world's greatest and most famous composers. In amongst the real names, dates and nationalities, are five phoneys. Can you spot them?

George Friedrich Handel (1685-1759) German

Johann Sebastian Bach (1685-1750) German

Franz Joseph Haydn (1732-1809) Austrian

Rudolph Von Smettow (1740-1801) German

Wolfgang Amadeus Mozart (1756-1791) Austrian

Hector Adolph Buzzi (1769-1812) Swiss

Ludwig Van Beethoven (1770-1827) German

Gioacchino Rossini (1792-1868) Italian

Franz Peter Schubert (1797-1828) Austrian

Mikhail Ivanovitch Glinka (1804-1857) Russian

Frederic Chopin (1810-1849) Polish

Franz Liszt (1811-1886) Hungarian

Richard Wagner (1813-1883) German

Giuseppe Pizzo (1813-1901) Italian

Johannes Brahms (1833-1897) German

Georges Bizet (1838-1875) French

Peter Ilyich Tchaikovsky (1840-1893) Russian

Arthur Sullivan (1842-1900) English

Igor Plinplonski (1850-1937) Russian

Gustav Mahler (1860-1911) Austrian

Richard Strauss (1864-1949) German

Kurt Barsolova (1864-1956) Hungarian

Jean Sibelius (1865-1957) Finnish

The Nelson Touch**

Admiral Lord Nelson is standing on top of his column in the middle of Trafalgar Square facing due West.

Given the instructions:
RIGHT TURN! ABOUT TURN! LEFT TURN!

which way would he end up facing?

SOLUTIONS ON PAGES 381 AND 382.

What and Where?*

Some of the world's most famous landmarks have got into a muddle here. Can you unjumble them and decide where you would have to go to find them.

1. The Leaning Tower of Bridge.
2. The Taj Falls.
3. Buckingham Needle.
4. The Niagara Grande.
5. The Eiffel Mahal.
6. The Great Building.
7. The Rio Tower.
8. The Golden Gate Pisa.
9. Cleopatra's Wall.
10. The Empire State Palace.

Dotty Problems**

Without lifting your pencil from the page and without going over the same dot twice, join these twenty-five dots with eight straight lines.

If you don't know what a rebus is, don't worry. U R never 2 old or YY 2 learn something new. My dictionary definition of a rebus is 'an enigmatic representation of a name or a word or a phrase by pictures or letters or numbers or other words or phrases.'

So if 'ime' is the rebus way of saying: 'Not before time', (i.e. No "T" before time). And this:

B
E

– is B on E or BONE!

Top Ten**

1. What's this?

ONE ANOTHER
ONE ANOTHER
ONE ANOTHER
ONE ANOTHER
ONE ANOTHER
ONE ANOTHER

2. Popeye would have loved this. What is it?

AC SP H

3. What is the name of this young lady?

MARY
2,000 pounds

4. This is a rebus fit for a court of law. What does it mean?

STAND   OATH
U   UR

SOLUTIONS ON PAGE 382.

5. Have you been to this play?

ADO

ADO   ADO

ADO   O   ADO

ADO   ADO

ADO

6. There are six letters here, all pointing to a cold climate. What are they?

WETHER

7. What word is this?

8. What does this mean?

STAND	TAKE	TO	TAKING
I	YOU	THROW	MY

9. Here is a well-known phrase. Can you spot it?

ONALLE

10. This is the alcoholic's lament to his bottle. Can you translate it into sober English?

OICURMT

Finally*

Rearrange these six letters and what do you find?

D E E H N T

SOLUTIONS ON PAGE 382.

SOLUTIONS

WORD PLAY

Mr. Thyme's Puzzle

'A nod's as good as a wink to a blind horse.'

Verbal Display

1. **To hustle** is to push and hurry.
2. **To brawl** is to fight.
3. **To gratify** is to please.
4. **To munch** is to eat.
5. **To repulse** is to drive off an attack.
6. **To submerge** is to go under water.
7. **To distort** is to put something out of shape.
8. **To meditate** is to think deeply.
9. **To wallop** is to hit someone or something.
10. **To somnambulate** is to walk in one's sleep.

Collecting Collectives

1. A shrewdness of apes
2. A cete of badgers
3. A shoal of bass
4. A sloth of bears
5. An army of caterpillars
6. A clowder of cats
7. A drove of cattle
8. A peep of chickens
9. A murder of crows
10. A dule of doves
11. A school of fish
12. A skulk of foxes
13. A gaggle of geese
14. A husk of hares
15. A cast of hawks
16. A brood of hens
17. A siege of herons
18. A haras of horses
19. A smack of jellyfish
20. A kindle of kittens
21. A deceit of lapwings
22. A leap of leopards
23. A pride of lions
24. A plague of locusts
25. A watch of nightingales
26. A parliament of owls

Homophones

1. a. Right b. Rite
2. a. Band b. Banned
3. a. Maize b. Maze
4. a. Assent b. Ascent
5. a. Foul b. Fowl
6. a. Pact b. Packed
7. a. Bowl b. Bowl
8. a. Ball b. Bawl
9. a. Seine b. Sane
10. a. Place b. Plaice

ANAGRAMS

Head Over Heels
Somersault

European Cities
1. VENICE   2. NAPLES

3. ATHENS
5. SIENA
7. PARIS
9. OSLO
11. LENINGRAD
13. OSTEND

4. REIMS
6. BASLE
8. CORK
10. ROME
12. TOLEDO
14. GENEVA

World Cities

1. MINSK
3. TUNIS
5. KABUL
7. SIMLA
9. RENO
11. SAN DIEGO
13. TIJUANA
15. TUCSON
17. MADRAS
19. MANILA
21. VALENCE
23. KYOTO

2. TULSA
4. LAGOS
6. SEOUL
8. LIMA
10. LAS VEGAS
12. DETROIT
14. TANGIER
16. TEHRAN
18. DARWIN
20. DENVER
22. VILNA
24. ACRE

Occupy Yourself

1. GAOLER
3. WARDER
5. AIRMAN
7. PRIEST
9. TAILOR
11. TRADER
13. DOCKER
15. WARDEN
17. MASON
19. DIVER
21. DYER
23. TEACHER
25. DENTIST

2. WELDER
4. HATTER
6. EDITOR
8. SINGER
10. DANCER
12. ARTIST
14. PARSON
16. TUTOR
18. NURSE
20. BAKER
22. ACTRESS
24. RAILMAN

You Name It

1. MEG
3. NEIL
5. ROSIE
7. LAURA
9. ETHEL
11. MABEL
13. DELIA
15. TESSA
17. RODNEY
19. GLYNIS
21. STEVEN
23. THELMA

2. DORA
4. MILES
6. RHODA
8. GRETA
10. EDGAR
12. MOIRA
14. CILLA
16. STELLA
18. GLENDA
20. MARTIN
22. INGRID
24. TERESA

Problematic Phrases

1. PARISHIONERS
2. FUNERAL
3. INFECTION
4. MISFORTUNE
5. STEAMINESS
6. ENDEARMENTS
7. HUSTLERS
8. WAITRESS
9. REMUNERATION
10. PUNISHMENT
11. VIOLENCE
12. FILLED
13. LEGISLATION
14. MILITARISM
15. FAMILIES
16. UPHOLSTERERS
17. DESPERATION
18. CATALOGUES

Presidential Poser

Ronald Reagan

Gladstone

We want a mild legislator; Will mislead a great town; Wit so great will lead man; A man to wield great wills.

One Over the Eight

A STITCH IN TIME SAVES NINE

Prime Poser

Margaret Thatcher

HIDDEN WORDS

Alpha Plus

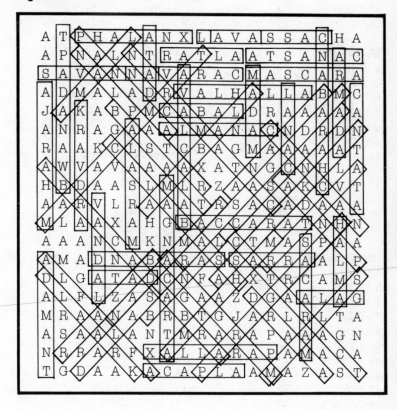

X-Tract

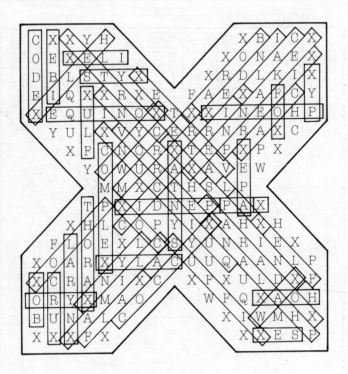

Quoting the Bard

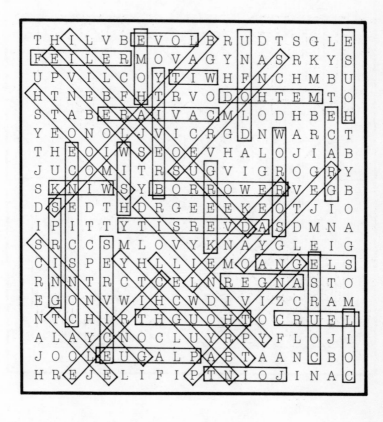

Parlez-vous?

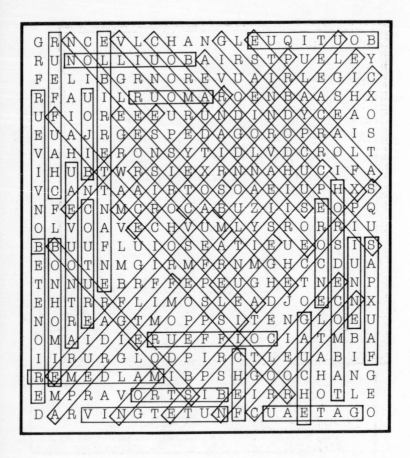

The Haystack

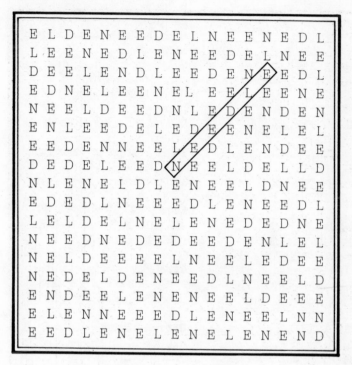

```
E L D E N E E D E L N E E N E D L
L E E N E D L E N E E D E L N E E
D E E L E N D L E E D E N E E D L
E D N E L E E N E L E E L E E N E
N E E L D E E D N L E D E N D E N
E N L E E D E L E D E E N E L E L
E E D E N N E E L E D L E N D E E
D E D E L E E D N E E L D E L L D
N L E N E L D L E N E E L D N E E
E D E D L N E E E D L E N E E D L
L E L D E L N E L E N E D E D N E
N E E D N E D E D E E D E N L E L
N E L D E E E E L N E E L E D E E
N E D E L D E N E E D L N E E L D
E N D E E L E N E N E E L D E E E
E L E N N E E E D L E N E E L N N
E E D L E N E L E N E L E N E N D
```

CIPHERS AND FRIENDS

Two of a Kind

1. JESUS CHRIST
2. SANTA CLAUS

The letters are exchanged for the ones that follow them in the alphabet. Hence, J becomes K, E becomes F, S becomes T, and so on.

Film Fun

1. THE SOUND OF MUSIC
2. ONE FLEW OVER THE CUCKOO'S NEST
3. THE FRENCH LIEUTENANT'S WOMAN
4. STAR WARS
5. SATURDAY NIGHT FEVER
6. EVIL UNDER THE SUN
7. CHARIOTS OF FIRE
8. SUPERMAN
9. ANIMAL HOUSE
10. FOR YOUR EYES ONLY

Word Numbers

1. RECTIFY
2. PATRIARCH
3. HERALD
4. GROTESQUE
5. VENTILATE
6. TREMULOUS
7. SNIGGER
8. REUNION
9. PROTEIN
10. MONSTROUS
11. LUMINARY
12. IDIOSYNCRASY
13. FRUSTRATE
14. DRAUGHTSMAN
15. DISTANCE

Novel Quiz

1. BLEAK HOUSE (Charles Dickens) 2. NINETEEN EIGHTY FOUR (George Orwell) 3. EMMA (Jane Austen) 4. JANE EYRE (Charlotte Brontë) 5. WINNIE THE POOH (A.A. Milne)
6. PERSUASION (Jane Austen)
7. THE TALE OF PETER RABBIT (Beatrix Potter) 8. FROM RUSSIA WITH LOVE (Ian Fleming)
9. FRANKENSTEIN (Mary Shelley) 10. LITTLE WOMEN (Louisa May Alcott)

Sounds Familiar

Have you any eggs? Yes we have eggs. Have you any ham? Yes we have ham. OK I'll have ham and eggs.

Mixed Faith

1. Well done thou good and faithful servant.
2. His banner over me was love.
3. I am that I am.
4. I am escaped with the skin of my teeth.
5. I came not to send peace, but a sword.
6. He that hath ears to hear let him hear.
7. He came unto his own and his own received him not.
8. Who against hope believed in hope.
9. What I have written I have written.
10. Let your yea be yea, and your nay, nay.
11. A man after his own heart.

False Start

ALL THE FIRST AND ALL THE LAST LETTERS ARE FALSE.

Vowel Play

PERSEVERE YE PERFECT MEN EVER KEEP THESE PRECEPTS TEN

Unnatural Break

ALL OUR LIVES WE ARE CRUSHED BY THE WEIGHT OF WORDS.

Alphabetical Extractions

1. Evergreen
2. Rhythm
3. Minimum
4. Quinquireme
5. Anagram
6. Nineteen
7. Gargling
8. Wigwam
9. Cyclic
10. Puppies
11. Kinky
12. Gypsy
13. Success
14. Xerxes
15. Thirty
16. Fanfare
17. Evasive
18. Suburb
19. Horror
20. Liable
21. Jazzy
22. Damned
23. Ululate
24. Jejune
25. Voodoo
26. Ironic

The Word

Excommunication.

E	10	100	0	1000	1000	UNI	100	AT	X	N
E	X	C	O	M	M	UNI	C	AT 10	N

Full Marx

You need the missing vowels, because with them you will have the titles of six of the Marx Brothers films: Animal Crackers, Monkey Business, Horse Feathers, Duck Soup, A Night at the Opera and A Day at the Races.

WORD CIRCLES AND LADDERS AND SQUARES

Word Circles

1. COERCION	2. SCIATICA
3. CYCLAMEN	4. BELIEVER
5. SYNDROME	6. EDUCATOR
7. ORIGINAL	8. HYSTERIC
9. HARMONIC	10. GARGOYLE
11. MYSTICAL	12. HACIENDA
13. MNEMONIC	14. METAPHOR
15. GLYCERIN	16. EULOGIST

Magic Spell

There are 1,024 ways to spell out **ABRACADABRA**

Six-Letter Odd-Ends

1. PAGODA	2. ASTHMA
3. CHERUB	4. ORCHID
5. PERIOD	6. ABSURD
7. ANNEXE	8. BEHALF
9. ENGULF	10. BORZOI
11. CUDGEL	12. FULFIL
13. CONSUL	14. RHYTHM
15. VICTIM	16. FATHOM

17. FLAXEN	18. SOLEMN
19. GAZEBO	20. STUCCO
21. ROCOCO	22. ~~STEREO~~
23. STUDIO	24. DYNAMO
25. CUCKOO	26. EMBRYO
27. BAZAAR	28. JAGUAR
29. METEOR	30. LIQUOR
31. ZEPHYR	32. CANVAS
33. HAGGIS	34. NOUGAT
35. LARIAT	36. CRAVAT
37. LANDAU	38. ORMOLU
39. CONVEX	40. GALAXY
41. CHINTZ	42. QUARTZ

Bird Fivers

Crane

In for a Spell

Ail, aim, bail, bilk, fed, fog, fop, for, form, gory, hilt, him, ilk, jab, jail, jilt, kilt, limn, milk, nog, prong, pronged, pyx, slim, slut.

Musical Spell

Fife, flute, lute, tuba, oboe, trumpet, tambourine, pipe, viol, viola, violin, drum, piano, gong, tabour, tabret.

Fill-ins

1. RAT	2. SAPS	3. CARES
ART	ASPS	SCARE
TAR	PASS	RACES
	SPAS	
4. RIPEST	5. TEAMS	6. POST
PRIEST	STEAM	POTS
SPRITE	MEATS	TOPS
	MATES	STOP
	TAMES	SPOT
7. POOL	8. MEAD	
POLO	DAME	
LOOP	MADE	

Word Ladders

1. PIG
wig
wag
way
say
STY

2. FOUR
foul
fool
foot
fort
fore
fire
FIVE

3. WHEAT
cheat
cheap
cheep
creep
creed
breed
BREAD

4. NOSE
note
cote
core
corn
coin
CHIN

5. TEARS
sears
stars
stare
stale
stile
SMILE

6. HARE
hark
hack
sack
sock
soak
soap
SOUP

7. PITCH
pinch
winch
wench
tench
tenth
TENTS

8. EYE
dye
die
did
LID

9. PITY
pits
pins
fins
find
fond
food
GOOD

10. POOR
boor
book
rook
rock
rick
RICH

11. TREE
free
flee
fled
feed
weed
weld
wold
WOOD

12. GRASS
crass
cress
tress
trees
frees
freed
greed
GREEN

13. FLOUR
floor
flood
blood
brood
broad
BREAD

14. TEA
sea
set
sot
HOT

15. MINE
mint
mist
most
moat
coat
COAL

16. BLACK
blank
blink
clink
chink
chine
whine
WHITE

17. WITCH
winch
wench
tench
tenth
tents
tints
tilts
tills
fills
falls
fails
fairs
FAIRY

18. WINTER
winner
winder
wander
warder
harder
harper
hamper
damper
damped
dammed
dimmed
dimmer
simmer
SUMMER

INTERNATIONAL WORDWAYS

Ici Français

1. See you soon.
2. Farewell.
3. Affair of the heart.
4. Trusted assistant.
5. In fashion.
6. Familiar with.
7. Ahead of one's time.
8. Exquisite miniature.
9. Love letter.
10. Tired of pleasure.
11. Decorative scroll or frame.
12. Everyone to his own taste.
13. Final blow.
14. Low cut of a dress.
15. Seemingly to have experienced before.
16. The right word.
17. Pseudonym.
18. Out of the ordinary.
19. Out of date.
20. Daring.

Hidden Countries

1. Iran, Vietnam
2. Malta, India
3. Sweden, Lebanon
4. Panama, Spain
5. Tonga, Togo
6. Lesotho, Ghana
7. Dahomey, Nepal
8. Peru, Uganda
9. Chad, Andorra
10. Gabon, Mali

Origins

1. French 2. French 3. Latin
4. Spanish 5. French
6. Italian 7. Latin 8. Arabic
9. Yiddish 10. Portuguese
11. Haitian 12. Polynesian
13. Swedish 14. Japanese
15. Hindi 16. Turkish
17. Hindi 18. Norwegian
19. Hindi 20. Greek
21. Latin 22. Greek
23. Greek 24. Spanish

Slang words

Whistle and flute (Suit),
Trouble and strife (Wife),
Rosie Lee (Tea),
Pig's ear (Beer),
Dolly varden (Garden),
Daisy roots (Boots),
China plate (Mate),
Butcher's hook (Look),
Bees and honey (Money),
Apples and pears (Stairs).

English Spoken Here

1. à la carte
2. à propos
3. bagatelle
4. bon appetit
5. bon mot
6. bric à brac
7. carte blanche
8. c'est la vie
9. clique
10. compère
11. coquette
12. crème de la crème
13. debût 14. faux pas
15. genre 16. mélange
17. piquant
18. tour de force
19. vis à vis 20. beau geste

Down Under

Aussie	Australia/Australian
Bathers	Swimming costume
Billabong	Pond
Bowser	Petrol pump
Bush (the)	Countryside
Cobber	Mate
Didgeridoo	Trumpet
Dingo	Australian wild dog
Dinkum	Honest
Duds	Best clothes
Goanna	Lizard
Good on you	Well done!
Grazier	Farmer
Gum tree	Eucalyptus tree
Jackeroo	Pupil on sheep/cattle station
Joey	Baby kangaroo
Jumbuck	Sheep
Lollies	Sweets
Milk bar	Dairy & general grocery shop
Moke	Horse
Noah's ark	Shark
Nong	Idiot
Paddy melon	Small wallaby
Pommy	Englishman/woman
Port	Suitcase
Postie	Postman
Sheila	Girl/woman
Swag	Bundle of belongings

SECTION 1

Spot the Difference
1. Shop

Spot the Difference
2. Fun in the Sun

Spot the Mistake
1. Bonjour

Apart from the apples instead of onions, both drivers are on the wrong side of the road and Marseille should be 650 kilometres from Paris.

Spot the Mistake
2. Cor Blimey!

It is 1953 but "Mary Poppins" was not on show until 1964, the Post Office Tower was built in 1965 and there was no Prince of Wales then.

SECTION 2

Spot the Difference
3. Departure Time

Spot the Mistake
3. Ex Libris

"Wind in the Willows" is by Kenneth Grahame, "Lord of the Flies" should be listed under Fiction and "Born Free" should be under Wild Life.

SHADOW SHOWS

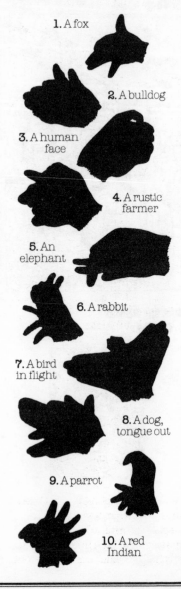

1. A fox

2. A bulldog

3. A human face

4. A rustic farmer

5. An elephant

6. A rabbit

7. A bird in flight

8. A dog, tongue out

9. A parrot

10. A red Indian

SECTION 3

**Spot the Difference
4. School's Out**

**Spot the Difference
5. Waiter**

**Spot the Mistake
4. Victorian Parlour**

**Spot the Mistake
5. Pharoah's Folly**

It's 1864, but Kipling was not born until 1865, there were no telephones until 1876, the song was not yet written and The Times only had classified ads on the front.

Hinges, power points and padlocks are all out of place in Pharoah's tomb, as are prehistoric cave paintings and Greek inscriptions!

NUMBER FUN

Twenty Questions

1. c	2. d
3. c	4. a
5. c	6. b
7. b and d	8. b
9. d	10. c
11. a	12. d
13. d	14. b
15. b	16. b
17. c	18. d
19. b	20. c

What Next?

a. 6   **b.** N (for Ninety)

c. 15

d. 5 (the numbers give the years of the two World Wars)

e. 35   **f.** T (for Ten)

g. 27

h. Any number at all: the numbers were picked at random and so there is no sequence!

Pick a Number

1. 1,000,000,000
2. 4,195 miles
3. 90,000,000
4. 40
5. 291,000,000
6. 1.6093
7. 4,700,000,000 years
8. 10,000m³
9. 1,000,000,000,000,000,000
10. 56m

Punch and Judy

Punch is 52. Judy is 39.

Monday to Friday

49

AD/BC

99 years old. There was no year 0.

Next Please

1. 31: the numbers are those of the days in the month, starting with January.

2. 48: the number doubles each time.

3. 1: the numbers are 1837 to 1901. The reign of Queen Victoria.

4. 65: each time you double the previous number and then subtract 1.

5. 9: each time two numbers are followed by a third which is the figure you get when the two numbers are multiplied together.

6. 1: the figures represent the number of times a clock will strike if it strikes once every half-hour as well as striking on the hour; the series here begins at 11.30.

7. 9: 1(+5 =) 6, 2(+5 =) 7. 3(+5 =) 8. 4(+5 =) 9.

8. 536: you must subtract 101 each time.

9. 8589934592: each number is multiplied by half of itself to form the next number.

10. 250: it's simply 1000 divided first by 9, then by 8, then by 7, then by 6, then by 5, then by 4.

Big Shot

Johnny who saw the smoke knew of it first; Bobby who heard the shot, second; and Willie who saw the bullet hit the water, third. Light travels faster than sound and sound faster than a bullet.

Now What?
20. The figures represent the coins and notes in the British currency from ½p to £20.

How Much?
£100

Where There's a Will
The widow would receive £205.13.

Not so Silly Willie
£10,737,418.24

Drink Up
£1 each. There was a grandfather, father and son.

The Lost Note
The cost of the room was £27 minus the £2, therefore £25. The error comes from mistakenly adding £27 and £2 and getting the misleading figure of £29.

Share Out
Alex will receive 2,500 pennies, Bobby 1,500 and Colin 700 pennies.

Bow and Arrow
The bow cost £20.50 and the arrow 50p.

The Pools Winner
£19,005

Auntie Nellie
£160

See a Man About a Dog
£49

A Pound of Apples
The two ways of selling are only identical when the number of apples sold at 30 for £1 and 20 for £1 is in the proportion of 30 to 20.

Inflation
£25.25; £28.25; £30.25; £36.25

Your Number's Up
The prices quoted were for house numbers at 12 pence per digit. A number 6 digit cost him 12 pence.

Mugger's Money
From Mr Ascot £88. From Mr Berkshire £44.

CLOCKING IN

Long Time
The faster watch gains on the slower one at the rate of three minutes every hour. After 20 hours, the faster one will be ahead by exactly one hour.

On Strike
300 times

Long Hands
55/143 minutes past 12 or 60/143
past 1.

Felines and Rodents
6 cats can devour 100 rats in 100
minutes (6,000 seconds)

Stitches in Time
18

Timetable
It was 5 and 5/11 minutes past
1 o'clock.

Party Time
It began at 59 minutes past ten. It
is now 54 minutes past eleven.

Digital Clock
0. The figures represent the
sequence on a digital clock
showing hour, minutes, seconds,
as one p.m. approaches.

13	3	14
11	10	9
6	17	7

Nine-a-side
This is how the butler did it:

3	3	3		4	1	4
3		3		1		1
3	3	3		4	1	4

Misplacement
The 7 and the 12 must be
interchanged.

Amazing!
The totals of rows, columns, and
diagonals is 19,998. The four
corners also total 19,998. The
amazing property is that if you
turn the square upside down, it still
works, each row, column and
diagonal will total 19,998.

MAGIC SQUARES

Quarter of a Century

9	11	18	5	22
3	25	7	14	16
12	19	1	23	10
21	8	15	17	4
20	2	24	6	13

Radioactive Problem
You need only move 3 containers.
Replace 6 by 3, and 9 by 6, and put
9 where 3 was:

CALCULATOR PUZZLES

Mini Quiz
1. $1815 \times 20 = 36300$
2. $36300 \times 31 = 1125300$
3. $1125300 \div 10 = 112530$
4. $112530 + 10,000,000 = 10112530$
5. $10112530 - 1805 = 10110725$
6. $10110725 \div 80 = \mathbf{126384 \cdot 06}$

Talking Calculators
1. 379919 2. 7105
3. 4509 4. 3704
5. 57738 6. 378809
7. 57108 8. 5355378

The Percent Puzzle

$0 + 920 - 156·25 + 129·78 + 3518·17 - 4414·08 + 666·66 + 1600 - 650 - 850 + 42·68 + 450·24 - 163·55 + 409·26 + 701·15 + 372·36 + 3055·25 - 3750 + 4907·25 + 1469·75 - 6561 - 1697·67 = 0$

To the Letter

1. 155,3125	2. 375
3. 787.5	4. 14,914285
5. 4.2777778	6. 2,111112
7. 0.52	8. 20
9. 123.09375	10. 107

Dictionary Digits

1. SOS	2. LOLLIPOP
3. BOGGLE	4. HI
5. HOHOHO	6. OBOE
7. HOG	8. EEL

Common Factor

1. 3784	2. 3159
3. 1395	4. 1827
5. 2187	6. 1435

In all sums the digits in the answer are the same as those in the multiplier.

Multiplication Digits

1. 1963		2. 198	
x 4		x 27	
7852		5346	
3. 1738		4. 159	
x 4		x 48	
6952		7632	

DIGITAL DILEMMAS

The Weigh In

One grapefruit weighs 600 gms

Add and Subtract

(a) $5 - 4 + 3 + 2 - 1 = 5$
(b) $2 + 2 - 3 + 4 - 5 = 0$
(c) $5 + 3 - 1 + 3 - 5 = 5$
(d) $12 + 3 - 4 + 5 - 6 = 10$

999999?

$99^{99}/_{99}$

Drunkards

$140 \div 3 = 46\frac{2}{3}$ days

Keep the Doctor Away

Benet ate 6 apples.

Tea Time

4 ounces

Bookworm

The important part of this problem is to remember how we stand books on a shelf.

The first page of volume 1 is indicated by the left arrow, and the last page of volume 6 by the right arrow. Beginning and ending at these points the worm passes through 10 covers totalling 30 millimeters, and 4 texts totalling 12 centimeters, for a complete journey of 15 centimetres.

Stick in the Mud

36 feet. One ninth (or

two-eighteenths) of the log was in the mud: 4 feet. Five-sixths (or fifteen-eighteenths) was above water: 30 feet. And 2 feet was in the water, making 36 feet in all.

Fishy Problem
45 pounds

Number Scrabble
17531908 + 7088062 = 24619970

Baby Monkeys
3 lbs

Farm Fare
3

Talking Turkey
20 kg

What's the Difference?
12 km^3

Two Dozen
22 + 2 = 24

Four Fives
$5^5 \div 5.5 = 6\frac{1}{2}$

Sum Subtraction

$$
\begin{array}{r}
555555555 = 45 \\
x \quad\quad 99999 = 45 \\
\hline
555455556 = 45
\end{array}
$$

Ten Not Out
T E N

Father and Son
80

Fowl-up
28 eggs

CONUNDRUMS

Value the Difference

Six dozen dozen = 864

Half a dozen dozen = 72

So the difference between them is
864 − 72 = 792

Family Problems

There are four boys and three girls.

Poor but Honest

1. So no one will ever find him out.
2. Because he's candid.
3. Chessman.
4. Because he only follows you in sunshine.
5. Ad-vice.
6. Time out of mind.
7. Because the heads were on the wrong end.
8. Spending one's last penny on a purse.
9. Because he is equal to any post.
10. Milestones, you never see two together.
11. A paying one.
12. Sarcasm.
13. Through the customhouse.
14. Give them chairs and let them sit down.
15. It is better not to get into a stew.

Brief Encounter

The Countess is Lady Constance's mother

Four of a Kind

Giggling

Poetical Problem

The first line of the verse gives you LAD, the second ADDER. The complete word is LADDER.

Easy

The letter E.

Which Way?

'Do you live here?'
If you are in Here the answer will be 'Yes,' and if you are in There the answer will be 'No' regardless of the man's residence.

Choral Conundrum

Anthem

Cat-astrophe

The same three cats.

Russian Riddle

Husband and wife.

Jumbled Letters

JUST ONE WORD

Aunts and Uncles

The boy is the man's sister's son.

The Whole Lot

None.

Revolutionary Conundrum

Saratoga (Sara-toga.)

False or True

The following statements are false:
1. Untrue
3. Untrue
5. No, he didn't
12. Untrue

15. The duck-billed platypus has.
16. No, it weighs 1¾ lb.
19. Untrue.
24. Wrong, there are 845!

All the others are true.

Three Dimensional Shapes
1. A and C   **2.** B
3. B   **4.** A
5. D

Before Your Very Eyes
The lines are all the same length.

A Question of Angles
The line A to C is the same length
as the one from B to D; it is the
angles that make them look
longer.

The Distance
The distance is the same.

A Matter of Size
The fields all cover the same area.

Curious Cube
The view of the cube could be from
above or below. The line is perfectly
straight.

Right Angles
Angles A and B are the same.

Key to the Problem
1. A and D   **2.** D and F
3. C and E   **4.** C and F
5. A and D   **6.** B and H

Triangular Terror
Thirty-five triangles.

The Mystery of the Sphinx

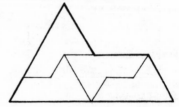

All Square

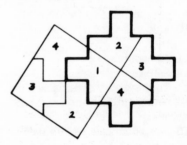

Square and Triangle
Fold the square in half and make
the crease FE. Fold the side AB so
that the point B lies on FE, and you
will get the points G and H from
which you can fold HGJ. While B is

on G, fold back AB on AH, and you will have the line AK. You can now fold the triangle AJK, which is the largest possible equilateral triangle obtainable.

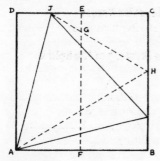

Paper Letter

It is the letter E.

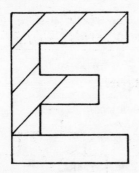

Folding an Octagon

By folding the edge CD over AB we can crease the middle points E and G. In a similar way we can find the points F and H and then crease the square EHGE. Now fold CH on EH and EC on EH, and the point where the creases cross will be the same as 1. Do the same to the other three corners and you will be able to cut out the octagon.

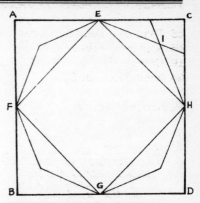

The Biggest Hole in the World

To do this, fold the paper down the centre and make several cuts from each side as shown. Then cut the doubled edge from A to B, leaving parts C and D uncut. The paper will now open up into a large ring.

Pinhole Puzzle

The second piece of card appears to have 3 dots too.

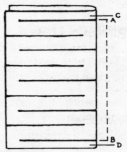

Quick Quiz

1. Albumen. If you've put yolk, you've spelt the yellow of an egg!

2. One.

3. A 50p piece and a 10p piece. One of them wasn't a 50p piece, but the other one was!

4. The letter S.

5. Incorrectly.

6. All twelve.

7. 202 each time!

8. 12, of course!

9. January 1st and December 31st fall in the same year every year.

10. Probably!

One Number

1

Unlucky Thirteen

R. All the others are the initial letters of the twelve months of the year.

Lewis Carroll's Puzzles

1. As curly haired James was sleeping in bed,
His brother John gave him a blow on the head.
James opened his eyelids, and spying his brother,
Doubled his fist, and gave him another.
This kind of a box then is not so rare
The lids are the eyelids, the locks are the hair.

2. That salmon and sole Puss should think very grand
Is no such remarkable thing.
For more of these dainties Puss took up her stand;
But when the third sister stretched out her fair hand,
Pray why should Puss swallow her ring?

3. Five seeing and seven blind
Give us twelve, in all, we find;
But all of these, 'tis very plain,
Come into account again.
For take notice, it may be true,
That those blind of one eye are blind of two;
And consider contrariwise,
That to see with your eye you may have your eyes.
So setting one against the other
For a mathematician no great bother
And working the sum you will understand
That sixteen wise men still trouble the land.

4. **1.** You are not a doctor.
   2. Dictionaries are valuable.
   3. Unselfish people do not save bottle tops.

5. 10 per cent

The Bridge Problem

Connie is the widow.

Death by Drowning

If statement 1 is false: murder but not by Bob.
If statement 2 is false, murder by Bill
If statement 3 is false: accident
This reveals that no two statements can be false. So either none or one is false. From 4, just

one man could not have lied. So no man lied. Since no man lied, it was suicide.

Marriage Lines

1. Mr Foyle's
2. Dark hair
3. Mr Foyle is bald.

Mad Cap

His reasoning was thus: if his cap were white, either one of his rivals would have known that his own was black, for the remaining man's raised hand showed that he saw a black cap, and that couldn't be this knight's if his were white. None of the other rivals dropped their hands to show they knew the colour of their own cap, which means his couldn't be white and therefore must be black.

A Hit or a Miss

If one missile has a chance of missing the target, then all 4 have a chance of missing. Also the target may be hit by 1, 2, 3 or 4 missiles, so Billy was wrong.

MINDBENDERS FOR MASTERMINDS

One Word

NOON

A Time Teaser

9.30

Letters Salad

I C A Z. The other letters read aloud all mean something (I see a sea, I see a bee, I see a jay, I see a ewe), but I C A Z means nothing.

What's Hot?

The sun.

Alarming

Only one hour and a quarter – because your alarm will have woken you at 8.15 that night!

Twin Twister

Jack and Jill are two children from a set of triplets.

Train Trial

The same place from which he jumped.

Charades

Banquet (Bank, wet)

Letter by Letter

All the words can be reduced by one letter at a time and form complete words all the way to a one letter word. For example, brandy, brand, bran, ran, an, a.

That's Cricket

Neither; they both average 3

Plural Puzzle

1. Daughters-in-law
2. Attorneys general
3. Brigadier generals
4. Judge advocates
5. Chargés d'affaires
6. Potatoes

7. Notaries public
8. Laws merchant
9. Opera
10. Pelves
11. Sergeants major
12. Teaspoonfuls
13. Piccolos
14. Tables d'hôte
15. Courts martial
16. Paymasters general
17. Messrs.
18. Mesdames
19. Crises
20. Men of war
21. Lieutenant colonels
22. Banditti
23. Cannon
24. Phenomena
25. Aviatrixes
26. Menservants
27. Oboes
28. Oxen
29. Valets de chambre
30. Data

Special Feature
Each letter of the alphabet appears 3 times.

Underground Stations
1. Westminster
2. Leicester Square
3. Euston
4. Victoria
5. Blackfriars
6. Tower Hill
7. Charing Cross
8. Baker Street
9. Kingsway
10. Green Park
11. Strand
12. Elephant & Castle

Beauty Queens
Caroline the blonde hairdresser is the oldest. Amelia the brunette receptionist comes next. Bernice the redheaded typist is next.

Find the Number
4368

All in the Family
1. 27 pairs of cousins.
2. 12 pairs of father and son.
3. 12 pairs of brothers.
4. 18 pairs of uncle and nephew.
5. 9 pairs of grandfather and grandson.
6. 13 people altogether.

Liquid Refreshment
First you fill the 3 pint container. Empty it into the 5 pint container. Fill the 3 pint container again. Empty it into the 5 pint container until the latter is full. Now one pint will remain in the 3 pint container.

MATCHSTICK PUZZLES

Triangular Trouble

1.

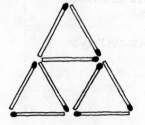

2.

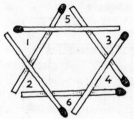

3.

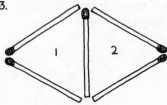

4.

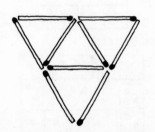

5.

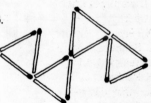

Matcho

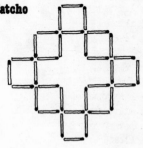

MatheMATCHics

1. NINE

2. IV + I = V

3. VII − II = V

4. VII − V = II

5. II − I = I

6.

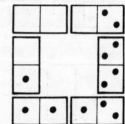

DOMINO PUZZLES

7. Look at it upside down

Untouchables

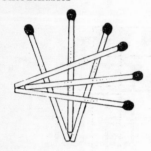

First Square

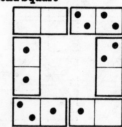

All You Need

Second Square

Long Division

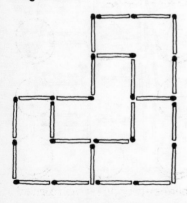

Triangular Terror

First Rectangle

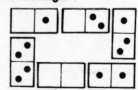

The Three Rectangles

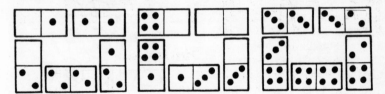

Giant Square

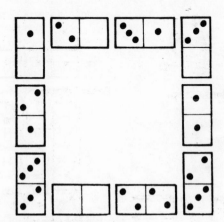

COIN PUZZLES

Cross Challenge

Square Challenge

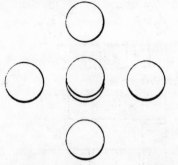

There are two coins in the middle.   There are two coins at each corner.

Circular Challenge

Here are your three moves:

1. Move 4 to touch 5 and 6
2. Move 5 to touch 1 and 2
3. Move 1 to touch 5 and 4

The circle should now look like this:

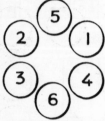

Pyramid Challenge

Here are your three moves:

1. Move 1 to below the bottom row and place it between and under 8 and 9.
2. Move 7 up two rows and place it to the left of 2.
3. Move 10 up two rows and place it to the right of 3.

The H Problem

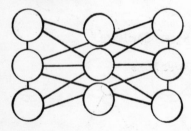

Sixteen Coins

Put your first and second fingers on the two asterisked coins and bring them round into the positions indicated by the dotted lines:

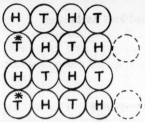

Now, with your fingers still on the same two coins, push the six coins (that's to say the three coins in the second row and the three coins in the bottom row) to the left and you will end up with the columns looking just as you want them:

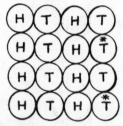

Six in a Row

Here are your three moves:

1. Move coins 1 and 2 to the right of 6
2. Move coins 6 and 1 to the right of 2
3. Move coins 3 and 4 to the right of 5

Eight in a Row

Here are your four moves:

1. Move coins 6 and 7 to the left of 1
2. Move coins 3 and 4 to the right of 5
3. Move coins 7 and 1 to the right of 2
4. Move coins 4 and 8 to the right of 6

Head Over Heels

Count always in the same direction, missing out one coin each time before starting the next count.

Nine-a-side

Here are twenty-eight coins in a square, with nine coins on each side. At each of the four corners to the square there are two coins and in the centre of each of the four sides there are five coins.

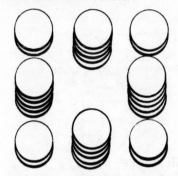

Here are twenty-four coins in a square, with nine coins on each side. The square is made up of eight piles of coins, with three coins in each pile.

Here are twenty coins in a square, with nine coins on each side. At each of the four corners of the square there are four coins and in the centre of each of the four sides there is one coin.

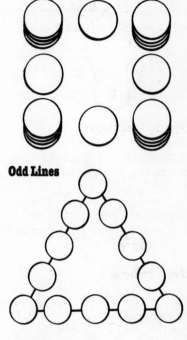

Odd Lines

Seven Rows

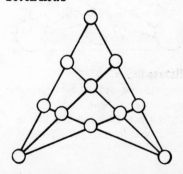

Nine Rows

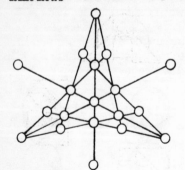

Twelve Rows

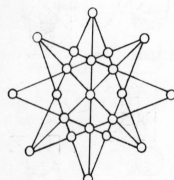

Fifteen Rows

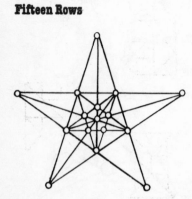

TANGRAMS

Shapely Tangrams

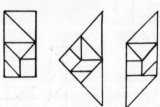

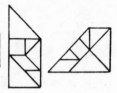

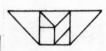

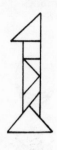

Number Tangrams

Alphabetical Tangrams

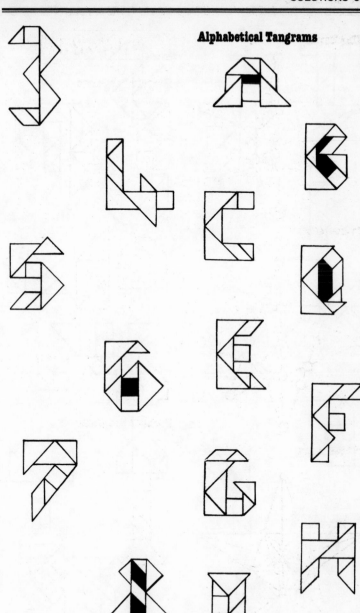

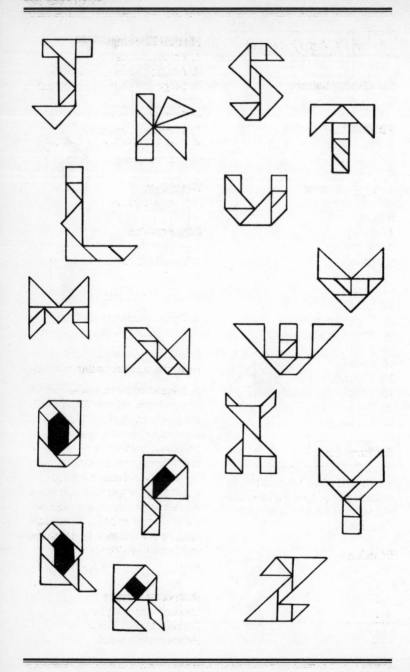

The Missing Letters
Q

What's What?
1. A bald head.
2. Tomorrow
3. Your breath
4. A pack of cards
5. The letter E
6. A sponge
7. Silence
8. Your future
9. A stitch
10. A hole
11. A pen
12. A coffin
13. Their own nose
14. A right angle
15. A candle
16. A kiss
17. A carpet
18. Down – like swan's down
19. The motorway
20. Holes

My Three Sons
Yvan. The Lawyer's name is 'bar' spelt backwards, the soldier's name is 'army' spelt backwards, so the sailor's name is 'navy' spelt backwards.

Oddition
```
  11
   1
   1
+  1
----
  14
```

Musical Meanings
1. **Presto** means fast.
2. **Adagio** means very slowly.
3. **Largo** means in a slow, dignified style.
4. **Fortissimo** means very loud.
5. **Dolce** means sweetly.
6. **Crescendo** means increasing the volume slowly.

Weak Word
Strengthlessness

Unpunctuated
1. He said that that 'that' that that woman said, ought to have been 'which'.

2. It was 'and' I said, not 'but'.

3. The murderer spoke angrily. Half an hour after he was hanged.

4. Time flies? You cannot. They pass by at such irregular intervals.

5. Esau Wood saw a saw saw wood as no other wood-saw Wood saw would saw wood. Of all the wood-saws Wood ever saw saw wood, Wood never saw a wood-saw that would saw wood as the wood-saw Wood saw saw wood would saw wood, and I never saw a wood-saw that would saw wood as the wood-saw Wood saw would saw, until I saw Wood saw wood with the wood-saw Esau Wood saw saw wood.

Composers' Corner
These are the five phoneys:
Rudolph Von Smettow
Hector Adolph Buzzi

Giuseppe Pizzo
Igor Plinplonski
Kurt Barsolova

The Nelson Touch

East. He begins facing West. Once he has made a right turn he is facing North. He then makes an about turn and is facing South. Finally he turns left and is facing East.

What and Where?

1. The Leaning Tower of Pisa – Italy
2. The Taj Mahal – India
3. Buckingham Palace – England
4. The Niagara Falls – USA/Canada
5. The Eiffel Tower – France
6. The Great Wall – China
7. The Rio Grande – USA
8. The Golden Gate Bridge – USA
9. Cleopatra's Needle – England
10. The Empire State Building – USA

Top Ten

1. Six of one, half a dozen of the other.
2. Spinach (sp in ach)
3. Mary Overton
4. You understand you are under oath
5. *Much Ado About Nothing*
6. A bad spell of weather
7. Continue (c on t in u)
8. I understand you undertake to overthrow my undertaking.
9. All in one
10. Oh, I see you are empty.

Finally

THE END

Dotty Problems

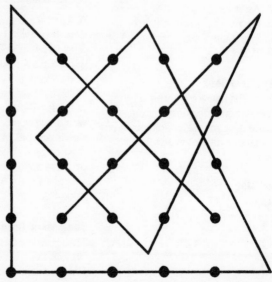